FEB 02 2010

Finding Anyone,

7/c

Anywhere,

Anywhen

Finding Anyone, Anywhere, Anywhen

Noel Montgomery Elliot

FIREFLY BOOKS

A FIREFLY BOOK

Published by Firefly Books Ltd. 2009

First printing

Publisher Cataloging-in-Publication Data (U.S.)

Elliot, Noel Montgomery, 1941–
    Finding Anyone, Anywhere, Anywhen / Noel Montgomery Elliot.
Originally published: Brampton, ON: Genealogical Research Library, 2005.
[320] p. : ill. ; cm.
Includes index.
Summary: Techniques for using the Internet to locate people who lived during any century in the past, as well as how to find people living today in any place in the world.
ISBN-13: 978-1-55407-470-9 (pbk.)
ISBN-10: 1-55407-470-3 (pbk.)
1. Genealogy—Computer network resources—Handbooks, manuals, etc. 2. Genealogy—Computer network resources—Directories. I. Title.
025.069291 dc22   CS21.5E555 2009

Library and Archives Canada Cataloguing in Publication

Elliot, Noel Montgomery, 1941–
    Finding anyone anywhere anywhen / Noel Montgomery Elliot.
Includes index.
ISBN-13: 978-1-55407-470-9
ISBN-10: 1-55407-470-3
    1. Web sites—Directories. 2. Internet searching. 3. Genealogy—Computer network resources. 4. Investigations—Computer network resources. I. Title.
ZA4201.E44 2009   025.04
C2008-907445-9

Published in the United States by
Firefly Books (U.S.) Inc.
P.O. Box 1338, Ellicott Station
Buffalo, New York 14205

Printed in Canada

Published in Canada by
Firefly Books Ltd.
66 Leek Crescent
Richmond Hill, Ontario L4B 1H1

The publisher gratefully acknowledges the financial support for our publishing program by the Government of Canada through the Book Publishing Industry Development Program.

Table of Contents

Introduction

In the beginning, our ancient ancestors created artwork and text, pictographs and hieroglyphics, and each created work was an original.

With the invention of the printing press, mass production of copies of any original work became possible. Creativity exploded worldwide. As costs came down, the ability of people to share art and printed communication created a virtual torrent of knowledge and information.

It is always the creativity of individuals—inventors, innovators and visionaries—that leads the way.

The invention of radio and television created instantaneous mass communication. Each broadcast meant that anyone with a receiver would receive a simultaneous copy of the original work. Recording devices allowed copies to be literally frozen in time, for later playback.

In 1958, Jack St. Clair Kilby invented the integrated electronic circuit, or microchip. His invention paved the way for the miniaturization of computers and the birth of the Internet. Once again, another creative individual influenced and changed the world.

And so it was with the invention of the popular personal computer or PC. The Apple computer, one popular example, was born in 1975. Two teenagers in California were largely responsible for its success.

The Apple was designed by Steve Wozniak to demonstrate to his local computer club, and when a store ordered 50 of them, he and his friend, Steve Jobs, began production. The Apple II and its clones revolutionized the lives of millions of people throughout the United States and Canada.

The low price of PCs brought them within reach of highly creative and talented young people in their teens and twenties. For the first time, the power previously available only to multinational corporations and governments was suddenly available to the public.

Apple computer clubs swept the continent. Here, in monthly meetings, computer enthusiasts could meet to excitedly discuss new ideas and try out new experiments and programs.

Still, one thing was missing. And that missing something created a truly formidable challenge.

These avid computer club enthusiasts and other PC users wanted to go far beyond their local clubs and neighborhoods. They wanted nothing less than to be able to communicate globally, and exchange ideas with other young people all over the world.

To do this, they needed to cross language and geographical barriers, and political boundaries. It also had to be free, or almost free. How on earth could all these creative people—potentially millions of people scattered around the globe—share information and communicate with each other?

A large part of the answer came during a remarkable four-year period, from 1991 to 1994. A visionary scientist named Tim Berners-Lee, working in Geneva, Switzerland, created a shared information space which allowed communication among a group of research scientists. These scientists needed the ability to retrieve information regardless of the variety of computer platforms that were in use at the time.

Berners-Lee's real intent, however, even in his first proposal in 1989, went far beyond the needs of the physicists he worked with. He envisioned nothing less than a worldwide communication system for public use. And from 1995 onwards, the World Wide Web literally skyrocketed in popularity.

True, there were many Internet protocols being developed as early as the late 1960s, particularly by the U.S. military, and small nets were being used at an early date. It was the public's demand, however, that exploded the Internet into the real global phenomenon it has now become.

Today, the distinction has become blurred between the Internet and the World Wide Web (www). In this book I will often use the words interchangeably, but generally speaking, the word Internet will always include the World Wide Web.

The idea of retrieving information was paramount for the scientists in Switzerland when the World Wide Web was born, and it is still paramount. Remember this: everything that we call human history is simply what individuals have done, whether they acted alone or in a group. And retrieving information about individuals, precisely and accurately, is what this book is all about.

The Internet opened up tremendous resources that are extending deep within all fields of knowledge. The most remote details from the ancient past are coming alive at an unbelievable rate. New discoveries in the present are being added as they occur. Timelines become blurred: the first part of this sentence is already in the past.

New information is accumulating at a stupendous rate. It cannot be fathomed by any one person. It is unprecedented. Nobody, not even governments, can stay on top of it.

Every day hundreds of millions of new facts become available. Those who delve too deeply into the information world find themselves speaking of a new disease – information overload.

This book is designed to provide you with the specific techniques that allow you to find and identify almost any individual, whether that person lived a hundred years ago, a thousand years ago, or even if that person is alive and living in our world today. This book will also provide you with the tools you need for navigation as the Internet unfolds.

You will also be sharing a vision of where the information highway is heading, what type of traffic it will have in the future and why.

To clearly see that future vision, we must first explore some unknown ancient history about ourselves.

This ancient history is quite well hidden. It is unknown to the vast majority of people in the world today. That, however, is all about to change.

Our Hidden History

Homo Sapiens at Dawn

The birth of modern man begins many thousands of years ago. Scholarly ancient history books along with recent archaeological discoveries have told us far more today than what was known just one generation ago. It is for certain, however, that our beginnings are rooted in small tribal groups or clans.

The members of these tribes are truly our ancient ancestors. If they did not exist, then we would not exist today.

Recent discoveries are making it clear, however, that if we do not relearn some basic truths about our ancient past, our civilization today will most likely collapse—not in some distant future like some have imagined—but perhaps within our lifetime. If society and governments incur great errors, it will be partly because we forgot where we came from.

Many historians have studied the differences between ancient tribes. Emphasizing differences is only half the story, however, and focusing just on differences alone may be misleading.

After all, if you focus just on the differences between you and your own siblings, without understanding the similarities and common elements, it might result in a fight. If we focus on differences only between nations, but without understanding, it could—and has in countless instances—led to war and destruction.

Instead of differences, let us look at the similarities between all of the ancient tribes, and see if we can pick up some new understanding. Remember: many of these tribes developed, seemingly unknown to each other, on several continents. And yet there were three major similarities between all of them. It is the similarities that provide important and crucial clues about our own nature, characteristics and origin.

1.   Kinship

All early tribes were characterized by a strong energy-bond we call kinship. Each member of the tribe felt a strong sense of belonging. They shared a powerful family feeling. This bond created a strong rapport and affinity between each member of the tribe. They knew how they were all related to each other. They understood this on very deep levels and felt that relationship emotionally. It was a constant.

2.   A Common Ancestor

Early tribes all carried, from generation to generation, the verbal story of a common ancestor. The common ancestor was seen as the tribe's founder, head or chief.

He was viewed as the ancestor from whom they had all descended. This shared belief strengthened the kinship feeling among every member of the tribe and provided a sense of purpose and value to the very existence of the tribe itself. Every man, woman and child felt this force: they had a common ancestor.[1]

3.   Shared Religious Beliefs

Shared religious beliefs, regardless of what other groups believed, acted as a unifying force, and strengthened the feeling of oneness among each member of the tribe. It also helped to ensure the probability and protection of their descendants.

The Rise of the Nation-State

As tribes grew larger and larger through the centuries, they would encounter other tribes, and if friendly enough they might coexist and engage in trade, or even form alliances against an invading tribe that appeared to be a common threat. Some encounters, however, were more like clashes, and the differences in beliefs and symbols spawned a multitude of rivalries, conflicts and wars.

Those that prevailed in wars, whether by physical might or intelligence, formed what we call nation-states. This led to formation of countries and nations, usually led by monarchs, demigods, emperors or dictators. The important thing to remember about this development is that the oneness or family feeling that previously was a common characteristic of each tribe was gradually displaced within this new framework of society. The feeling of kinship declined as nation-states continued to move aggressively up through the hallways of time and into the future, eventually reaching what we now call our lifetime.

Now we have arrived in our present world. Countless conflicts are going on around the world. We sense many threats to our future existence. Yet these impending threats are mixed in with the hopes of the majority of people who wish for a more peaceful life in the future, along with reasonable prosperity.

It is during this time, in just slightly more than a decade, that the Internet has flourished. Like any new tool or invention, it has the potential for great harm, or great benefit. It really depends on how it is used.

The Internet is part of the new media along with television and a plethora of electronic gadgets.

> The media forms our new community. The electronic village is our hometown. . . . We know celebrities but they don't know us. The new community is not a reciprocal neighborhood like earlier ones. These vicarious relations help create *a new kind of*

loneliness—the loneliness of people whose relationships are with personae instead of persons.[2]

The Discovery of Ebla

Ebla is typical of the archaeological discoveries that keep changing our previous concepts about early civilization and bring a wealth of new information to light.

For 15 years archaeologists had been digging in the mounds of an ancient civilization on the plain of Syria. The dig took place between ancient Egypt and the Mesopotamian empire.

Then, in 1968, the archives of an ancient city-state were unearthed, revealing 15,000 clay tablets covered in an unknown cuneiform writing. At first, none of the experts were able to translate the writing, even though there are almost 7,000 known living languages in the world today.[3]

A little later, the archaeologists made yet another fortunate discovery. They found a unique set of tablets within the archive that showed the unknown Eblamite words along with the equivalent words in Sumerian.

By good fortune, Sumerian was a language that was understood by language experts. Suddenly they had the key to understanding this unknown language.

Incidentally, these translation tablets formed the oldest dictionary or lexicon ever discovered on our planet.

Armed with the key to deciphering the Eblamite tablets, the experts began the unprecedented task of translation. No archaeologists had ever encountered 15,000 clay tablets that required translation.

In the words of Dr. Giovanni Pettinato, an expert in ancient languages who had participated in the Italian Archaeological Mission in Syria,

> All the other texts of this period recovered
> to date do not total a fourth of those from
> Ebla.[4]

A remarkably clear view of daily life in ancient Ebla began to unfold. The records being translated cover trade, commerce and the historical chronicles of this ancient empire. The details include over 5,000 geographical place-names. In essence, Ebla is rewriting much of history in that part of the ancient world.

Among thousands of people recorded in the tablets is the name of David, which has never been found in such ancient texts except the Bible. The large number of genealogical references include the names of Abraham, Esau, Saul and a King Ebrium, who was believed by some scholars to be Eber, the great-great-grandson of

Noah. Ebla's scribes had even kept track of the names of the people just traveling through their country.

In the Old Testament of the Bible, the Book of Deuteronomy refers to Abraham's grandfather as being a Syrian. These discoveries have excited and mystified scholars of Judaism, Christianity and Islam, and have left historians thinking anew about the formative years of ancient civilization.

Although the discovery of Ebla is fascinating, it is just one of a multitude of other discoveries coming to light all over the world. Some recent discoveries are nothing short of astonishing.

For example, more than 400,000 fragments of scrolls, books and papyrus were found in a 30-foot deep city dump near Oxyrhynchus, an ancient provincial capital in Egypt that dates from Roman times. Some of these fragments are more than 2,000 years old. Another large deposit of fragments from an ancient library has also been found in Herculaneum. The fragments are covered with grime, soot and ash—the result of volcanoes and fires.

Now, thanks to NASA technology and innovative scientists, enhanced multispectral imaging allows researchers to see through multiple layers of these fragments, even black upon black layers, to actually see the original writing clear enough to read, reconstruct and recreate as modern images.

Texts from these two cities now being translated include property records, New Testament epistles, early Islamic writings and fragments of lost plays by Euripides, Sophocles, and unknown works by the most famous classical writers and poets of antiquity.[5] Only 20 years ago many historians would have thought such scientific achievements were utterly impossible.

Many of the missing pieces of our true and ancient history are now coming to light. The shape of history is altering so quickly and on such a large scale that the authors of our history books are hard-pressed to stay abreast of the changes that follow each new major discovery.

Let me put it this way: the new revelations of science and archaeology require constant updating of our textbooks if we are to live in an aware and educated society.

The Discovery of Cousinhood

Consider this opening phrase of a poem published in 1670 by John Wilmot:

The world appears like a great family.[6]

Later, in 1839, William Blackstone published a classic work entitled *Commentary on the Laws of England.*[7] In his research, he had noted that we all have a surprising number of ancestors.

For example, you have two parents, different from each other, or you would not exist.

It would seem logical to assume that your two parents each had two parents also, and therefore you have four grandparents. And you might further assume that your four grandparents each had two parents, and so on.

Your ancestors seemingly double with each generation as you go back in time. And although this may seem very logical and correct, it is actually not true! In fact, it's impossible. You can prove it to yourself in a few minutes.

Take a calculator and keep doubling your ancestors every 28 years or so (an average generation) and before you can get back to 2000 years ago, your ancestors outnumber the total world population at that time! And remember: we're not talking about anyone else – just your ancestors! The truth is, human history is loaded with cousins marrying cousins, far beyond what most people would ever imagine.

Mathematicians, genealogists and other scientists have examined this apparent enigma and have come to one conclusion: many of your ancestors knowingly or unknowingly married their cousins. This resulted in a reduction in the number of ancestors from the usual rate of expansion.

Genealogists call this phenomenon pedigree collapse. Pedigree collapse appears to have first been mentioned in a paper by Robert C. Gunderson.[8] It means that our ancient family trees are much smaller than we used to believe. As well, these repeated marriages between related cousins are far more plentiful in the past than we ever imagined. Parts of our ancestral family tree had branches that were expanding at a normal rate while other branches were contracting by comparison.

Certain individuals may show up in your family tree more than once. Acknowledging these events is the only way to reconcile world population with the fact that we each have two parents.[9]

In a more extreme example, the marriage of a brother and sister has quite a dramatic effect. This happened in some royal families, for instance. When a brother and sister marry, then there are only the same two people as parents for both of them in the previous generation, not four.

Often, because of religious and cultural beliefs, known sexual liaisons between certain individuals with their cousins were kept quiet and were closely guarded secrets. Genetic evidence is changing all that.

Far more children were born out of wedlock than our parents and grandparents ever would have believed. In fact, many of our parents and grandparents simply wouldn't want to believe that this happened so often. This is understandable. After all, there was no convincing evidence of this reality until recently.

A term I particularly dislike is the word illegitimate when applied to children. Any child born into this world is as legitimate as any other child, and the use of the term illegitimate is of ill intent and demeaning and should never be used.

It would be more appropriate to refer to the activities of a parent of the child as engaging in illegitimate activities, contravening their vows or disrespecting social norms, but the child is not guilty of anything.

Today, DNA evidence and the human genome project have led to much closer linkage and cooperation between two very complementary sciences: genealogy and genetics.

While scientists may continue to argue about the exact and final degree of relationship, it is evident to them that everyone in the world is related. The relationship between us all is very clear:

We are all cousins

Many scientists now estimate that no person in the world could be further apart from you than 50th cousin. Other scientists believe that nobody else in the world today could be any further apart from you than 32nd cousin. But they all agree on one thing: that we are cousins.

You may ask, "Does this include all of the various races besides my own?" The answer is an emphatic yes. Yes, it includes all so-called races. No exceptions.

Even remote tribes are not really being discovered for the first time. They are only being rediscovered a very long time after they were separated from other ancient tribes. In more ancient times they had ancestors in common to us all. And the latest evidence still indicates the origin of our species took place in Africa and spread out from there to other continents.

The most remote tribes are part of the overall human gene pool. In their ancient history they were inter-mingled with other tribes and had common ancestors with them before being cut off through exploration, natural catastrophes or other events.

When you hear news about a remote tribe being discovered, remember they represent those more distant 32nd or 50th cousins. They are cousins greatly removed by degree, but nevertheless they are still our cousins.[10]

As Guy Murchie pointed out, each one of us has ancestors that include:

... all the blacks, Chinese, Arabs, Malays, Latins, Eskimos . . . who lived on Earth around AD 700.[11]

On a very positive note, another author, Alex Shoumatoff, had this to say on the subject of cousinhood:

> The political implications of this great kindred are quite exciting. If all of us could be made aware of our multiple inter-relatedness, if the same sort of altruism that usually exists among close kin could prevail through the entire human population . . . [our] differences . . . would seem secondary.[12]

It is evident as we look at today's world that the knowledge about our ancient kinship feelings and our beginnings are unknown to the vast majority of people.

It is also evident that most people are unaware of the vast wealth of names of people and places being unearthed in ancient archives every year.

Many of the tribes existing today pass along vast genealogies of their ancestors orally. They are recited aloud, from the eldest to the youngest. Now these genealogies are being recorded and documented by the younger generations. This is all possible with modern tape, CD and DVD recording devices and with video cameras.

Vast archives in the Vatican contain details about millions of people who lived during past centuries. They wait for their reawakening to be acknowledged in the world of digital data. Other religious institutions have contributions to make as well. We're waiting for them too.

However, the biggest unknown fact is still this: all of the people who ever lived in the past, along with everyone alive today, are cousins.

The fact that these things are unknown produces the exact opposite effect of what was true of our ancestors who lived in those ancient tribes: most of us don't feel any kinship feelings with people of different nationalities. Most of us only feel kinship for a very few of our own nationality. We have lost that kinship feeling, that oneness feeling, that should exist within mankind.

As a result of this lack of knowledge, we are obviously paying the consequences right now. The consequences are wars, genocide, starvation, disease, murder and other atrocities. In truth, our ignorance is working against the probability of our own future existence.

Are we not aware of the 2,000-year-old expression,

A house divided against itself cannot stand?[13]

What Creates Prejudice?

If you think about the fact those millions of ancestors lead precisely and directly down through the centuries to you, you may begin to change some of your built-in assumptions. Try to imagine for just a few minutes the range and kinds of people your ancestry includes.

Your ancestors include criminals, nobility, royalty and scoundrels of every kind. Remove just one of them from your ancestry and the you that is you right now, would not even exist. Give that realization a few minutes of your time. Refresh your memory screen.

Genealogical Bridges

Anthony Wagner is well known for his essays in the genealogical interpretation of history. In his scholarly book, *Pedigree and Progress,* he explains how occurrences that took place centuries ago are now emerging as major genealogical landmarks when viewed from today's vantage point:

> In the year 1265 a nephew of Kubla Khan, Emperor of China, married the half-sister of a Byzantine Emperor, who in 1279 married the sister-in-law of a nephew of St. Louis, King of France, and of Eleanor of Provence, Queen of England.[14]

This meant that 700 years ago a genealogical bridge was connected across the continents of Europe and Asia in less than 15 years, and through only eight people.

This is just one example of the countless thousands of genealogical bridges creating interlinkage between races, nations and countries throughout the course of human history. Every living person today is the result of common ancestry and genealogical bridges.

I remember vividly an incident that occurred when I was invited to speak to a group of students in a school in Ontario.

While talking about cousinhood I noted that these young children were absolutely fascinated. Then, during recess, one of the teachers asked me to come outside to the schoolyard where the children were playing. She told me how one of the girls that had been in my class had run out to all of her friends and blurted out excitedly: "Did you know we're cousins?" They all clustered around and were still talking about it excitedly when I arrived.

I began to wonder at that point, "What if all children, in every country were actually taught this when they were young?" I think the change would be enormous, and when these children reached university age, they might take their professors and leaders to task for not understanding how this really changes everything.

Could world wars develop if everyone had a kinship feeling for all ethnic groups? Wouldn't we instead rely far more on understanding, reasoning, negotiation and real diplomacy?

Keep these discoveries in mind as we progress.

As the full implications of these discoveries are assimilated, our basic and fundamental ideas about ourselves and our relationships with each other must change.

Our educational institutions, by definition, should be the early transmitters of these new perspectives, but not by boring and repetitive lecturing. Instead:

> Teaching is now understood as mature assistance to youthful learning, or self-teaching. . . . The teacher becomes a part of the learning group, sharing his greater maturity and knowledge, but seeking out ways of assisting others to learn rather than going through an empty ritual of forced feeding.[15]

With the essence of this chapter in mind, we will now step into the Internet world and lock-in on the single most important search technique we need to find the proverbial needle in the haystack.

NOTES

[1] Cheyne, T. K. (D.D.), and Black, J Sutherland (LL.D), (Editors) *et al, Encyclopaedia Biblica,* The MacMillan Company (NY) and Adam and Charles Black, London, 1899.

[2] Pipher, Mary. *The Shelter of Each Other: Rebuilding Our Families,* New York: Random House, 1996.

[3] See www.nationsonline.org.

[4] P. 735, "Ebla, Splendor of an Unknown Empire", *National Geographic* Magazine, (*National Geographic* Magazine, Vol. 154, No. 6, December, 1978, published by the National Geographic Society, Washington, DC.

[5] Gugliotta, Guy, "Imaging Technology Makes Ancient Text Readable", Washington Post staff writer, *Washington Post* (www.washingtonpost. com), May 30, 2005.

[6] Wilmot, John, Earl of Rochester, *Like A Great Family,* 1670.

[7] Blackstone, William, *Commentaries on the Laws of England,* The Clarendon Press (Oxford University Press), Occana, NY, 1969.

[8] Gunderson, Robert C., "Tying Your Pedigree into Royal, Noble and Medieval Families". Senior Royalty Research Specialist, Family History Library, Salt Lake City, Utah.

[9] *The Mountain of Names, A History of the Human Family,* by Alex Shoumatoff, 1985, A Touchstone Book, Simon & Shuster, NY.

[10] *Are You and I Really Cousins...or...How Many Ancestors Did We have in A.D. 1 and in 1700 B.C.?* by Arden H. Braeme, Jr. II, OAE, Published *in The Augustan Society Omnibus Book 7* (1986), 74-78. Robert L. Cleve, Ph.D., OAE, KCR, Chairman of the Board, The Augustan Society, Inc, kindly supplied this article.

[11] Murchie, Guy, *The Seven Mysteries of Life: An Exploration of Science and Philosophy,* Mariner Books, 1999, pg 344ff. ISBN 0-39595-91-5

[12] *The Mountain of Names, A History of the Human Family,* by Alex Shoumatoff, 1985, A Touchstone Book, Simon & Shuster, NY.

[13] Abraham Lincoln, quoted in his speech of June 6, 1858. Origin: *The Holy Bible,* Matthew 12:25, when Jesus is recorded as saying "Every kingdom divided against itself is brought to desolation; and every city or house divided against itself shall not stand".

[14] Wagner, Anthony, *Pedigree and Progress: Essays in the Genealogical Interpretation of History,* Phillimore & Co., Chichester, England, 1975. Page 72.

[15] Giles, Harry H. "Order and Pattern in Successful Teaching", from *The Educational Trend,* December 1954. Also quoted by Morse, William C. and Wingo C. Max, *Psychology and Teaching,*

The Internet Unfolds

When the Internet began, it is important to know that there was an immediate need for convergence. By this statement, I mean that text alone, without diagrams, images, pictures and photos, wasn't enough.

Several centuries ago, the brilliant educator Comenius created a breakthrough in teaching and wrote a revolutionary book entitled *Orbis Pictus* (*Pictured World*). It was the first picture-book or illustrated manual of instruction for the young. It was published at Nuremberg, Germany in 1657.

> Comenius, with the instinct of a great teacher, felt that to give words without things (pictures) to the pupil was not simply to retard his progress, but to lay the foundation of vague and inaccurate conceptions.[1]

Another educator, Pestalozzi, ventured further by trying to have the actual object in front of the child learning the word—and from these two educators "flowed the excellent custom of *giving object lessons in infant schools*".[2]

Object lessons and show and tell sessions are still used today in virtually every school. These techniques are tried, tested and proven to more clearly communicate ideas, topics and personal experiences.

And so it was that the Internet also needed, right from the beginning, a convergence of images, pictures, and text to bring about a clear understanding through this new communication medium.

At first, websites sprang up more or less helter-skelter and confusion abounded. One of the main challenges was how to find the website that actually had the information you were looking for.

This led to the natural need for massive indexes to the data held on various websites. Ideally, these indexes would guide researchers to the right place where they might find the proverbial needle in a haystack.

If you know the history of nonfiction books to any degree, one of the most basic requirements is an index, especially when complex terminology is used throughout the book.

Remember: a noun is the name of a person, place or thing. Historically, our libraries always had card catalogs in the past, and many still do.

These card catalogs were essentially indexes to the book titles and subjects in a collection, and of course, the authors had to be indexed by name as well. And books about geographical regions, different languages or from different countries had to be specified and grouped together.

What happened in the history of books is very similar, in part, to what has happened—and is continuing to happen—on the Internet.

If we look at the history of books themselves, certain kinds of books were really indexes with data attached. Some of the major ones are:

Dictionaries
Lexicons
Encyclopedias
Bibliographies
Concordances
Directories

The Internet has many advantages over books, however, because once books were reproduced digitally, computer programs could be written to cross-reference information in ways never before possible with books in libraries.

On the Internet you can search many encyclopedias for free. One of the best free encyclopedia websites will even let you participate in creating this marvelous resource. Take a look at the following website available in 10 different languages:

http://wikipedia.org

Every word written in a book or on a website could be part of an index, and cross-referencing and sophisticated crisscross indexing became the major centerpiece of what are now known as search engines.

In 1962 the visionary Marshall McLuhan stated:

> When millions of books can be compressed in a match-box space, it is not the book merely, but the library that becomes portable.[3]

In the near future, most libraries will expand to become virtual libraries on the Internet. At first, catalogs will go online, and then their older and rarest books along with high-demand books. Once the data on the pages of these books has been digitally converted, then it can be shared globally. Best of all, this can be provided to anyone at very low cost, and in many instances for free.

In the future, our descendants will likely have library buildings filled with physical books in their pioneer villages, showing future citizens what life was like during the early 2000s !

More and more libraries are being transported onto the Internet to become virtual libraries. These virtual libraries are indeed portable, whether the data covers a dozen books or a million volumes. Books that were rare and locked in climate controlled glass display cabinets in the past, will be available to anyone, anywhere and at anytime they wish.

One choice for users will be to view scanned images (photographed pages) of books showing them as they were originally. Many researchers need to see the original work and form. This is particularly useful for rare books, artwork, maps and illustrations.

Another choice will be viewing the digital data that provides the user with the informational content, but not the original appearance or form. These are digital books.

Digital books are highly useful for many reasons, such as changing the font type and size and republishing a book that is in the public domain (not under copyright protection). Many older books were in very tiny type sizes, making them difficult to read. Now such works can be available in very large easy to read fonts.

In the Western Hemisphere, Johannes Gutenberg invented the printing press with removable metal or wooden letters in 1436. China had already been printing on a press using moveable hardened clay letters since 1041, although printing in China had begun long before that, during the 800s.

Then, in the 1960s, along came offset printing or instant printing, using photo-typesetting, and a new revolution was born.

Suddenly a photograph could be made of a rare work of art, and that photograph could be impressed electronically on a metal or paper plate. Thousands of copies could be produced automatically and instantly without the need of any typesetting.

Many collectors of rare original artworks and maps panicked at first, because they were afraid that if someone took a picture of their rare masterpiece, the value would be diminished.

Some purists felt that since early offset printing was inferior in quality compared to the original artwork, it would cheapen everything. They were all wrong.

Suppose you were a stamp collector, for example, and you possessed a very rare stamp worth $100,000. Someone could take a beautiful, high-resolution digital photo of that stamp and the photo might be worth a few dollars, but it is the original stamp that is worth the $100,000.

Offset printing, by producing prints and copies of rare art, created two marvelous benefits for both collectors of rare art and the public at large.

First, everyone, even the poor and middle classes, could afford a copy of a rare piece of art, and appreciate and enjoy it in their own home.

Second, as millions of people shared the appreciation and beauty of rare art, the value of the originals actually went up. As more new people acquired wealth for the first time, they had a new awareness of great art through seeing prints and pictures of it. Owning an original was highly desired, especially by the nouveau riche. Today, investing in original works of art is a huge field and prices continue to escalate over time.

Once again, the old marketing truths of supply and demand were working, but in a new way.

It is important to realize that nobody told the public to buy this great reproduced art. People just looked at the prints and were internally motivated within themselves to acquire a copy or print. Just the exposure to art itself motivated the public to buy.

Stores selling prints were simply displaying what was available, but not dictating what the public should like. Observant storeowners quickly became aware of what the public wanted.

I think one of the great errors of our time is marketing people who try to dictate or limit the choice of the public through strident advertising and controlled distribution. Just show us everything available, and we will choose what we like. It's just the way it really is.

The Information Highway

The time we live in has often been called the Information Age and we are truly witnessing nothing less than an information revolution. While there is an overwhelming explosion of data worldwide, wisdom is needed to find our way through this overwhelming morass of data. We need to hone in on our specific objectives and goals without getting totally lost in a never-ending and expanding universe of data.

Careful search techniques can locate information in minutes that may have taken many decades to find in the past.

For the most part, governments are rightly avoiding direct taxation of Internet users. The invention and use of the Internet was always premised upon it belonging to the people. Nevertheless, governments are very tempted to tax, especially in countries where the level of greed of those in control rises above the people's primary needs and rights.

When radio was first invented, the government stepped in and required everyone who wanted to own a radio receiver to purchase a license from the government. Just listening to a radio in your home in the 1920s required a radio license. A little experience with the public reaction to licensing led government officials to drop the idea very quickly decades ago.

Incidentally, speaking of radio, did you know that many elements of the Internet came from the hobby of amateur radio or ham radio? This fraternity of people talked on short-wave radio to others in every country of the world, long before the Internet was invented. They created and coined the word "net" where people clustered together on the air to discuss popular topics in a unique and invisible information space.

It was ham radio operators who created and operated the first radio and television broadcast stations.

They assisted people to make free telephone calls between countries even as early as the 1950s, using phone patches, an elementary forerunner of VoiP technology today.

If we look back now to the information highway, we see that the highway is the actual infrastructure of the Internet itself.

Picture in your mind a complex web of millions of highways with turnpikes, intersections or hubs. Websites are like tourist attractions along the way. There are stores, businesses, services, libraries, malls and thousands of other travel stops en route. You can tour or be a sightseer, or you can go instantly to any destination.

The big difference between the Internet versus cars on a highway is that you can move along the information highway to your destination at almost the speed of light: 186,000 miles per second. And gas prices aren't going up!

It's not just information, it's instant information. Distant websites on the far side of the planet seem to be as close as websites next door to us, and as faster Internet access speeds prevail, these huge distances and faster speeds seem to merge or collapse, and they soon become meaningless.

In our minds, whether we are conscious of it or not, we experience time and space disappearing, or becoming the same thing.

This merging of time and space can actually create a growing psychological challenge for children raised from birth in the first Internet-only generation in history.

If young children are dominated by only the Internet and games, it can become increasingly difficult for them to clearly distinguish between the invisible Internet world and the real three-dimensional world where their physical bodies live and breathe and where they must learn to interchange and socialize with other children. This is a new and vital challenge for our educational systems and social scientists.

Let's look at the builders of the information highways. Building this immense highway system requires a huge investment by many large and small corporations. Why are they spending so much money? You need to know. It is the power of our needs that really dictates what is happening. This is the single biggest clue to understanding how the Internet will develop in the future.

Billions of dollars have being spent so far on building the information highway. Why? That enormous amount of money is being invested because the investors expect trillions of dollars will be made in the future from its existence. That is, of course, only if those investors make the right choices. And who determines the right choices? We do!

No planners build highways unless they assume from the beginning that there will be a lot of future traffic. Traffic on the Internet consists of digital bytes and bits, whether it is emails, video, audio, games, movies, search engine queries or anything else. It's all just one thing: traffic.

The benefit for us? Wise members of the public can get huge benefits for no cost or very little cost, by doing some careful thinking and a little research on their own. Let's start right now.

Search Engines

Whether you are searching for someone in the past, or someone living today, the first essential tool on the Internet is a search engine. Everybody knows about them, but the majority doesn't really know the best way to use them.

When Internet novices first locate a search engine, the majority of them just type in a word or phrase, click enter and wait. That is often a great waste of time and can bring frustration and despair. Let's understand what these search engines are and how they work.

Search engines are websites that contain powerful programs called databases. A database stores information in such a way that any piece of information can be quickly retrieved through an elaborate system of indexes and related links.

Database websites can be contained on a single computer (a server) or on a large number of computers (server farms).

These powerful servers take in your request for information, search their internal database indexes, and serve back the results of your search request. Ebay and

Amazon, for example, use huge numbers of servers or server farms to handle auctions or sell books, videos and all kinds of other products.

Search engines began in the 1990s. Many of the early search engines were created as university research projects. Many students and university researchers had the foresight to see our future needs and they also had the knowledge and creativity to write programs to meet those needs.

Major search engines today such as www.google. com can handle millions of transactions in less than a second, for people requesting information at the very same moment from all over the globe. It is no wonder that when Google went public in 2005 it was the largest public offering of its kind and raised $2.7 billion dollars from the public and institutional investors.

Currently Google has billions of web pages in its index, and it is constantly growing.

Google has big plans for the future and their researchers and developers have already turned out new resources that are highly useful, as well as beta or test versions of new databases and programs they are working on. You can stay on top of their research work by going to http://labs.google.com

When you search on most search engines, they currently show the first 10 or more websites matching what you seek—but—the first 10 are often those websites that have the most links to them from other websites. Usually the first links are sponsored links that pay the search engine owner for positioning near the top.
These first results may contain what you're looking for, but if not, there are ways around this to locate a site you may wish to find. The website you seek may purposely not have many links from other websites, or they might not be able to afford to pay Google for high ranking as a sponsor or advertiser.

Some current search engines are:

> www.google.com
> www.yahoo.com
> www.c4.com
> www.altavista.com
> www.lycos.com
> www.ask.com
> www.dogpile.com
> www.hotbot.com
> www.clusty.com
> www.msn.com
> www.kartoo.com
> www.ixquick.com
> www.gigablast.com
> www.teoma.com
> www.alltheweb.com

www.infospace.com
www.killerinfo.com
www.A9.com
www.scholar.google.com
www.findarticles.com
www.newspaperarchive.com

Some search engines require memberships. Some search engines search several other search engines, which can save time especially if the subject you are researching is relatively rare.

It is important to realize that search engines do not search genealogy databases, or any other databases that require memberships and passwords.

In fact, there are some websites that have no home pages at all, and contain databases known only to a select group of people. Most of these are not included in search engine results. These kinds of websites are part of what has been called the dark Internet or hidden Internet. It's likely that much more data may be within the hidden Internet than the visible Internet we're already familiar with.[4]

In general, powerful databases are structured in such a way that they can only be used by members possessing valid usernames and passwords.

So, even if a membership database contains millions or billions of names, you cannot determine what names are in there unless you are at that website. Sometimes you can carry out a free or limited search without being a member.

This is why websites containing databases should be visited and utilized if they cover the people and time periods you seek. A search engine can find the home page of these websites, but you must click on the link provided by the search engine to go there and check it out. That's part of researching.

There are very useful websites that list the many different types of search engines available. Some of these specialize in various subject fields of endeavor. Check out www.allsearchengines.com. Another website that compares search engines is:

www.searchengineshowdown.com

The main point to note is this: search engines differ from what was previously possible with printed books in the past, because they multiply a millionfold the ways of finding out information about anyone, anywhere, at any time period in the past and present.

A logical question might be, "How do search engines gather up such vast amounts of information?" Do they employ an army of people indexing information for them? Not at all!

Computer programmers create digital robots—known as robots or crawlers—that roam around the World Wide Web visiting every website they can to index the home page and other pages on websites where they are not blocked.

Every moment of every day these crawlers are tapping into new and old websites to gather up information. The crawlers convey the newly found data to the home website, where it is integrated into the ocean of data that's already there. The ocean just grows and grows.

At the search engine's home, every word is indexed except for words like "the", "and", etc. In other words, they are primarily looking at nouns, the names of people, places and things.

Search engines churn out their data in a similar form to concordances. That is, if you are searching for a particular person, place, or thing, search results will usually provide you with the name of the subject you seek within a sentence or two taken from a website source.

This way you have the word within the context of a sentence. This triggers your mind to select the most likely source for the information you seek, even when many sources come up in the search.

Usually the most relevant results come up first, but as mentioned above, some search engines and directories will show or highlight their paid advertisers first, along with heavily linked websites.

This often means that cluttered websites having links to, or ads for, many other websites may show up with higher priority than the website that you may wish to find. However, many websites prefer not to clutter up their sites with a lot of links and ads. A lot of clutter looks unsightly and unprofessional.

When I began using the Internet, I remember looking up the word genealogy on a search engine, and I was truly astounded to see there were over 10,000 responses. I was astounded because in the early 1990s genealogy wasn't exactly a household word.

Today, when I search for the word genealogy on a popular search engine, I get almost 80 million hits or responses! Initially, on the surface, that might seem wonderful, but in fact, it reveals a huge new problem facing researchers. Who can look through 80 million responses? Instead of too few facts, suddenly there are too many facts to go through!

Search Engine Techniques

I mentioned earlier that beginners often go to a search engine, type in a name and wait for the results.

Sometimes even people using the Internet a lot do little more than just type in what they're looking for. That is most often a big mistake.

For example, I went to Google[5] and entered my name, *Noel Elliot*. I got back almost two million results.

However, as soon as I put quotation marks around my name, *"Noel Elliot,"* I got back about 3,500 results.

Quotation marks are widely used by search engines to mean the results must be precisely the words or phrase between the quotation marks.

I got almost two million results on the first search because the search engine—if I just enter *Noel Elliot*—will look for Noel Elliot but it will also look for any website page that mentions Noel and Elliot even if they are widely separated in an article.

So remember this: if the name you are searching for is rare or uncommon, then using quotation marks will bring back comparatively few entries.

However, this doesn't work very well for common names. For example, if I choose the name *"John Smith"* within quotation marks, I get over five million results.

However, if I add a middle name, *"John Maynard Smith,"* I get less than 75,000 results. It turns out that someone famous had that name. But if I add the name Elliot as the middle name and search on "*John Elliot Smith*," then I get only 74 results. Obviously this name is not as famous. Experiment, experiment!

Here's another angle. I tried entering my name without quotation marks plus the word genealogy and Canada, like this: *Noel Elliot genealogy Canada*. I got 14,600 results. Even that is a lot better than the two million results I got when entering my name without the words genealogy and Canada.

One more step: if I enter "*Noel Elliot*" *genealogy Canada*, I get only five results. This is just a small sampler of how you can narrow down the results of a search.

A little ingenuity, thought and experimentation will convert a beginner to at least an amateur in a very short time. In today's world, a search engine is the primary resource for every kind of research.

This simply means that search techniques have to be constantly refined in order to precisely find the person you are searching for.

I strongly recommend that when you visit a search engine website, take the time to click on advanced search. Examine all the options very carefully and you will be richly rewarded.

You will be pleasantly surprised what search engine administrators have organized to refine your search immeasurably. Search engine operators spend a lot of time and energy to try and clearly illustrate what is now possible.

One last trick that you find very handy is to specify a range of years. For example, if I search *"JohnSmith" born 1617...1618* I get only 122 results. So, even with a popular name like John Smith, the search can be narrowed down b naming the year(s) of probable birth, marriage or death. When you specify a range of years such as 1617...1621 the search will bring back results only within that specific range.

NOTES

[1] H. T. Peck, Editor-in-Chief, *The International Cyclopaedia, A Compendium of Human Knowledge,* Vol. XI, Dodd, Mean & Company, 1898, page 30 (emphasis mine).

[2] *Ibid,* page 30.

[3] McLuhan, Marshall, *The Gutenberg Galaxy*, University of Toronto Press, Toronto, 1962.

[4] Stewart, Alan, "The Hidden Web" (insert), "Genealogical Googling", *Family Chronicle* Magazine, July/August 2005, page 28.

[5] This search was done on October 13, 2008

Finding People in the Past

Onomatology to the Rescue

Onomatology, or the onomastic sciences, are certainly not familiar words to the public. However, if you are seeking to extend a genealogy into the past, these relatively unknown sciences eventually become essential.

Broadly speaking, onomatology is the classification of names and their meanings, alternate spellings, origin, history and so on. You could sum it all up as the study of names.

Onomatology deals with the proper names of people, places and things. This science encompasses real names as well as fictitious names. It even includes the study of coined and invented names often used in fiction novels.

A certain group of researchers within this unusual science might specialize in just one specific type of names, such as surnames. Others focus on name changes, and yet others focus on aboriginal and native names. And we should all be very glad that this science is old and well established, because it becomes indispensable as we go back in time.

In China, where surnames are much older than in Europe and North America, there were originally just about 1,000 surnames. Compare that with more than 750,000 surname variations in Europe and the British Isles!

Legal Name Changes

Onomatologists and genealogists are concerned with name changes. For example, one person immigrating into Canada from Europe changed his surname from Pslajavicoski to Jacosky.[1] Fortunately, onomastic scholars documented this change, otherwise it might be very difficult for anyone, generations later, to trace their family tree if they were unaware of the name change.

Another publication provides a dictionary of over 30,000 Ukrainian surnames in Canada.[2]

When legal name changes are made in Canada, they have to be published in the provincial Gazette. This means there is always a place where investigators can find legal name changes. Fortunately, genealogists and onomatologists sometimes publish indexes to these gazettes, a few of them cover periods up to the mid- to late 1900s.[3]

Illegal Name Changes

Now picture this imaginary scenario: let us suppose two brothers, more than a century ago, had a serious argument over religion. That was not unusual at that time.

Let us further imagine that the argument got so intense the brothers decided never to speak to each other again, and they each decided not to let their wives or children associate with the others family.

One brother might change the spelling of his surname to clearly distinguish himself as if he was of a different family and therefore he no longer had any obvious association or connection with his brother's family household.

Each brother might raise their children to avoid the other family entirely, or imply that there is something unspeakably bad about the other brother's family. Later, as the remote brother and his family had almost faded from memory, if asked about the other part of the family, the one brother might say something vague, suggesting perhaps that there is a black sheep in the family.

One brother might move his family far away. Again, this is not as rare as you might think, especially in times past. Generations later, when the descendants try to trace their family tree, they would hit a brick wall. Over the years I have found some of these cut off families, and usually, the descendants on both sides no longer feel the need to allow an old argument to cripple their kinship now, a century later.

The old arguments might have been seen as very serious breaches a few generations ago, but they no longer are seen as grounds for breaking up a family and keeping descendants separated today. They become reunited. Stories like this are not all imaginary. Stories similar to this happened all the time in the past, and to a much lesser extent it still happens today.

Immigration

For other name changes, let's take a closer look at those who immigrated to North America in the past.

Occasionally, some overseas emigrants purposely spelled their names incorrectly. Perhaps they were a young couple fleeing parents and family in Europe or the British Isles. Perhaps their parents gave strict orders that for whatever reasons they could never see or marry each other. History has hundreds or perhaps many thousands of stories similar to this.

For a young couple in love, fleeing to North America for land and opportunity was their way out of family rules that were simply too strict to bear. Naturally, such a young couple would want to make sure they couldn't be found as they began their lives in their newly chosen homeland.

Sometimes immigration officials themselves simply copied names down incorrectly. Usually the spelling was subject to errors anyway, because it was often based on the way the name was pronounced verbally and how the officials interpreted the sound of the name when writing it down. And here we must point out that just as recently as 50 years ago, phonics was being taught in all our schools. People would hear a name spoken aloud, and then try to spell it based on their knowledge of phonics.

Phonics produced a generation of people who could spell very well, but no one method alone is perfect. Add foreign accents and poor pronunciation into the equation and it's easy to see why census-takers and immigration officials could easily make mistakes.

It is also true that there were good census-takers who were careful and meticulous, and there were poor census-takers in a rush to get home, didn't care much for the job, etc. Not much has changed!

Particularly in the earliest years of immigration, it was easier to slip undetected through the record-keeping process. No papers, or forged papers - thousands entered North America this way. And yet, the more onomatologists and genealogists work together, even these name changes can be figured out, mainly by a process of elimination, often on first names or later documents of marriage, census or taxation.

In general, professional genealogists have up to 21 ways around a genealogy block in the mid to late 1800s.

Familiarity and the study of surnames and given names by onomatologists provide us with reference books that often provide a breakthrough in tracing names that have changed over time. These reference books belong on the shelf of every serious genealogist.

Criminals

Others immigrating into North America were criminals, intent on doing anything they could to create an alias or false surname. This might work well until the time of marriage, since that particular record usually required the parents' names of the bride and groom, and required witnesses who provided their names and addresses. Often people trying to hide their identity would give some correct names, or parts of names, on such a document.

There are several other ways of tracing these purposely changed names that are very sophisticated. These techniques are known primarily to highly innovative genealogists and private investigators versed in an intense process of elimination and other methods, some of which may occasionally extend into gray areas.

A very few generations later, however, descendants of criminals might run into serious health problems if they cannot get a medical history of their ancestors to assist them in their own medical diagnoses. This means that one result of hiding your identity is that your descendants' lives could be at risk.

Fortunately, DNA and the genetic sciences are advancing to the place where even those who do not know their family ancestry can be assisted, and more so with each passing year.

Is Singapore Ahead of North America?

In the year 2000, Singapore became the first country in the world to conduct their entire population census on the Internet.

Think of the great savings and efficiency over door-to-door enumerations and all the paperwork and voter-machine problems.

Every citizen in Canada has a Social Insurance Number (SIN) and every citizen in the U.S. has a Social Security Number (SSN). Computers love to crunch numbers and they can do it instantly. What on earth are we waiting for? Maybe our governments should be humble enough to inquire from Singapore about their methodologies.

Another pleasant surprise on my trip to Singapore was the way in which they kept new or changed phone numbers instantly up-to-date. A screen on your telephone stayed up-to-date as a directory for the whole country.

This makes we wonder: How many trees do we cut down every year to produce telephone books? And we have to wait a year to get a new replacement for our current books. And the beat goes on. *Waste of time. Waste of money. Waste of natural resources.*

And think about all those trucks that are loaded down with heavy telephone books, bound in huge groups and dropped off at apartment buildings, condos, businesses and homes by a small army of people hired to deliver them.

Let's consult with Singapore!

Genealogists to the Rescue

Genealogy is classified two different ways—first, the "-ogy" ending tells us it is a science of something—and that something is genus, or generations, or human genesis.

Genealogy is the science of identifying an individual, in relationship to other family members. It uses the evidence generated by direct family connection of siblings, parents and so on.

As mentioned earlier, the science part of genealogy is becoming more closely linked with another science, genetics—the science where the chromosomes and the DNA molecule are being unraveled and accelerated.

In the great classification of things, genealogy is not only classified as a science on its own, it is also seen as an auxiliary branch of history. Genealogy provides the skeleton of family history. It is important to keep this duality—genealogy and history—clear in your mind, even though we will deal primarily with the science of genealogy in this book.

Genealogy has to do with a lot of investigative techniques, the outcome of which should provide documentary evidence. These source documents and findings provide a picture of a series of sharp occurrences between the cradle and the grave, and associations with close family kin.

A very large percentage of biographies begin with details about the grandparents and parents, and other family members, otherwise we would not understand the background, the challenges, and the kind of environment the subject was raised in during their formative years.

Genealogy is always a search for truth. It separates family mythology and family fiction (and sometimes over-inflated egos) from the reality of events as they really occurred. In this sense, genealogy is refreshing, for it teaches us that every family has ups and downs during the many generations that take place over a long period of time.

The person who really spotted and predicted the popularity of genealogy in the future, was Léon Roy, an archivist who worked in the Archives of the Province of Québec, Canada.[4]

The records of French Canadians are among the best in the world, if not the very best. In Québec, genealogy is often more than just a hobby or pastime—it is a passion.

Some of the largest family reunions in the world take place in Québec. It has been stated with authority that the greatest national treasure of Québec is their genealogical heritage. Their records are simply the best of any state or province in North America.

This is particularly fortunate for many American families in New England, New York, Michigan and all the northern border States who descended from the French. It is very common to trace such families back into the 1600s and beyond with relative ease, since links are most often provided to ancestors in the ancestral villages and parishes in France.

Since the French have spread out into every province in Canada, it is also fortunate for Canadians who have some French ancestry, including the Métis and the Acadians.

Remember the Roots television series craze that swept North America and then Australia? More people watched the television mini-series than watched man's first step on the moon.

Years later the Roots television production was selected by the Chinese government to be their New Year's special program, and it was seen on national television across China.

I tried to imagine the likelihood of the story of a black man's ancestry from Africa, as told by a descendant generations later in the United States, being used as an example and inspiration for the people in China. Since it was for the Chinese New Year, perhaps it was chosen by the government to motivate the people of China to view their future with optimism. I think it worked!

Anyway, during the Roots publicity, the fascinating thing to me, and mentioned in a great many magazines in the 1970s, was that all the so-called experts didn't see it coming. The public's interest in genealogy had been growing uphill in strength and numbers every year since 1960, but the experts didn't even see it happening as any kind of significant event.

All along, I kept thinking: Here is a hobby that is growing dynamically. Millions of people are strongly interested and excited. Nobody told the public to get interested in this hobby, no government told the people to do it, no advertisements told the public to get interested in tracing your family tree.

This is very important! Why? Simply because it shows that this phenomenon was a natural inborn need rising to the surface in people's lives at this particular time in history. It was all part of a search for identity and meaning in a society that was in danger of becoming rootless. It was some kind of natural response to the times we were living in and the conditions we felt around us.

And yet, it remained seemingly undetected for decades, even by the so-called social scientists.

The only people who really knew it was happening were those who were working in archives, because each year they needed more money and time to meet the swelling demand for information. For example, in their annual reports year after year, the Nova Scotia Archives referred to the huge backlog of mail, and asked other archivists how they coped with the rising tide of requests.

Genealogical societies and many historical societies were beneficiaries of this rising public interest in genealogy. Word of mouth played a large role until the media caught on. The ongoing interest in genealogy led to a swelling of the ranks among genealogical and historical societies. More and more clubs and family associations sprang up.

Each genealogy group had a library of helpful books, or used the local history collection of their public library. More and more books were being published, especially in the awakening period from the 1960s to the 1990s. Printed indexes to census records, birth records, baptismal records, tax records, voters' lists, immigration lists, city, town, township and county histories, sprang up everywhere.

Avid genealogists and historians came out in droves to genealogical society meetings. Societies held fairs and other meetings, drawing the public. Later, in these huge annual events, people crowded around the publication displays searching for books of interest.

In my mind, the most valuable indexes combine many indexes from different types of sources, in different periods of time, into one massive alphabetical index.

For example, in 1984, The Genealogical Research Library produced a three-volume set of books titled *People of Ontario 1600-1900*. It had been derived from a large number of publications and historical property maps, and thus Ontario was the first province to have an index combining a multitude of sources into one large index. It had been produced using the Apple II computer, machine-language programs, a disk operating system and a library of 5" floppy diskettes.

By the 1990s after upgrading the indexing programs and training scores of indexers, the library published 12 volumes, which covered all of Canada for three centuries of time, 1600-1900.

By the year 2000, the data in those books and new indexing had reached the place where even 84 huge volumes wouldn't contain all the data, and so the library decided to begin development of a major database engine for their website, www.grl.com.

Here's a personal way I can truly illustrate the huge advantage of the Internet over a library of genealogy books.

Let's compare the previous printing of the 12 books in the 1990s, with the Internet databank which came online in 2003.

The original 12 volume set of books published in the 1990s cost over $1000 to purchase. They held details of about two million ancestors.

Today, just ten years after those books were published, for a very few dollars, anyone can join the library at www.grl.com and search 21 million records. Add to that one million source document images that are available as well. These images can be downloaded for free by members. And then add to that, several thousand antique maps of every country in the world. The maps are also available to members.

The cost has dropped to a tiny fraction of the cost of the 12 volumes, while the amount of data available has increased dramatically on the Internet. Plus source images and maps. Additionally, a search on the Internet takes a fraction of a second, far faster than you can open a book and even begin to look.

Two Major Commercial Databases in the U.S.

In the U.S., there are two huge genealogy websites that are commercial in nature, namely, www.ancestry.com and www.genealogy.com. Both of these are databases owned by The Generations Network (previous known as www.myfamily.com). Both databases charge for most of their services on a database by database basis or by specific collections. Examine the content carefully to discern which database you need before paying any money. I advise people the same way about the database at www.grl.com.

It is always sensible to see if you can find what you need for free, before paying to search a fee-based website. Ultimately, you may indeed find that some fee-based sites are highly useful for finding what you're looking for and there are often many benefits to membership.

Most fee-based websites keep people employed who are excellent indexers—and they can be fired if their error-rate is not kept at a minimum. Other websites may have volunteer indexers providing the data, only to discover they have a mixture of correct and incorrect data. There are good indexers and there are indexers that are not so good.

In summary, there are advantages and disadvantages of fee-based as well as free websites, so the onus is on you to search carefully.

Cyndi's List

For the record, a popular website for locating genealogical websites has traditionally been Cyndi's List at www.cyndislist.com. While I still use this website, personally I liked the older layout this site had a few years ago. For me, I found the old listings quicker and easier to use than the current layout. However, that said, it is still the #1 index to genealogy sites and it is a primary resource and many researchers use it.

The largest database in the world, however, is absolutely free to search. And that database—surprisingly to most newcomers—is contained in two Mormon church websites, as follows:

www.familysearch.org
http://pilot.familysearch.org/recordsearch/start.html#

If you are searching for your ancestors I suggest you start with the free searches. If you are unsuccessful, then try the commercial searches, especially if they give you a free search or trial period to see what they have.

There are thousands of free databases. We have listed a few thousand of them in the Worldwide Website Directory at the end of this book. For example, most state and provincial archives have a website where more and more material is becoming searchable. They range drastically in the amount of information available.

About the World's Largest Free Genealogy Website

As mentioned, the single largest sources of free genealogical records in the world, is found at the Mormon church websites mentioned above. As more records are indexed around the world, they are moved into the free online database at www.familysearch.org.

Interestingly, this huge website and search engine is operated by the Church of Jesus Christ of Latter-Day Saints or Mormons as they are popularly called. I myself am not a Mormon, but they have made a huge impact on genealogical research globally. Again, the Mormon website at www.familysearch.org is the single most important website on our planet for finding free genealogical information.

The genealogy data includes the famous IGI or International Genealogy Index, which is a tremendous resource for genealogy for a large number of countries.

Let me get the legal niceties covered here: this website is owned by The Corporation of the President of the Church of Jesus Christ of Latter-Day Saints, Inc. The website's copyright ownership is vested in Intellectual Reserve, Inc., and the International Genealogy Index is a trademark owned by Intellectual Reserve, Inc.

The IGI lists millions of births, christenings, baptisms and marriages in countries around the world. Since a great many of these records are obtained from parish registers, the IGI is very valuable because in such cases, these are records of primary evidence.

The Mormon IGI is particularly strong in certain countries including the United States, England, Wales, Scotland, Mexico, Ireland, Germany, Austria, Canada and Russia.

The IGI records that were used to produce the indexed database were all microfilmed originally. These microfilms of scanned documents are stored in massive vaults in the mountains near Salt Lake City, Utah, within atomic bomb proof facilities containing a fresh water supply in the event of a catastrophe or war.

For the Mormons themselves, the acquiring and storage of these records is a necessity for church work by their members. You might notice that the IGI index is devoid of death records and cemetery records, and that's because of certain beliefs held by Mormons. When it comes to birth, baptism, christening and marriage records, however, they are loaded.

The Mormons also maintain their internationally famous Family History Library in Salt Lake City. This facility is a place not only used by researchers in the U.S., but by visiting researchers and scholars from many other countries as well.

The Mormon website also has another set of free records that are indispensable if you are searching for people who lived during the 1800s or early 1900s in England, Wales, Scotland, the United States and Canada. These are the every-name indexes to federal censuses. They've had very popular census records indexed for many years now, specifically:

1881 census of England, Wales, and Scotland
1880 census of the U.S.A. (all states)
1881 census of Canada (all provinces)

The 1881 censuses mention every family member, household by household, who was alive in those years. They include the name of every man, woman and child. Their ages are given, along with birthplaces, occupations, marital status and many other important facts as well. Every month more census records for various years are being added country by country.

In the Worldwide Website Directory included in this book, I have also listed many other websites providing various census years for different countries, some as early as the 1600s and others as recent as 1945.

This book is not meant to be a training manual for genealogists. A discussion of tax lists, school censuses, assessment rolls, cemetery records, burial records, wills and a plethora of other kinds of records is beyond the scope of this book. However, the Worldwide Website Directory will link you to these kinds of records and much, much more.

I will, however, discuss two particular areas here that are more specific to Internet searching. Let's discuss that old standby, newspapers, and kick it up a notch or two.

Newspapers

One of the sources for births, marriages and deaths— as well as millions of articles and social columns that might mention the people you seek—are newspapers.

Newspapers were being printed long before vital records of births, marriages and deaths were being collected by governments. Some newspapers published extensive genealogies of families who were early settlers.

The *Yarmouth Herald,* for example, located in Nova Scotia, published vast genealogies of New England families that had branches of the family who came to Canada.

The collected genealogies from the *Yarmouth Herald* were eventually published between the years 1896 and 1901. These comprehensive genealogies included detailed listings of families, generation by generation, often beginning in the 1600s and ending in the late 1800s. These newspaper genealogies were compiled into a massive book and published in 1993.[5] This book contains invaluable genealogical data for those seeking ancestors in the New England states as well as in Nova Scotia. The descendants of these families today are scattered throughout many other regions of the U.S. and Canada, and probably in a great many other countries as well.

In the Worldwide Website Directory you will find newspaper websites for about 200 different countries. You can investigate these on your own as well.

You will find almost every country listed and the principal newspapers, along with links to connect you directly to the particular newspaper you seek. Many of the newspapers have email addresses included in these listings.

If you are searching for a lost relative and you know they lived in a certain city, why not write a letter to the editor? It's free, and thousands of people have found missing family links by taking this simple step. Today you can contact editors by email, avoiding the cost of postage, envelope and a drive to the post office.

Digital Newspapers and Indexes

Wouldn't it be nice if you could search for anyone's name ever mentioned in a newspaper over a 40 or 50 year period? Or a century? It's here already!

Several groups around the world are scanning old newspapers and using highly sophisticated OCR (optical character recognition) software to convert old newspapers into digital data. Once digitized, other software creates indexes on any noun mentioned.

This is a researcher's dream come true, or at least it's becoming more true with each passing month.

One of the first companies that caught my attention near the beginning of newspaper digitization was *Cold North Wind, Inc.,* and I have followed their progress with great anticipation.

Their website is at www.paperofrecord.com. They have digitized well over 21 million newspaper pages at the time of writing. Newspapers in many countries are being digitized. This is necessarily a pay site, but well worth the money if you see newspapers in their list that you need to search.

Another website, www.newspaperarchive.com, claims to have 993.6 million articles covering 771 cities, over a 240 year period, and 2,975 titles, as of the time of writing. I searched on a rare name to sample the index and got several hundred hits. Again, this is a subscription site.

Also of particular interest to genealogists is the website http://www.genealogybank.com/gbnk/

At the time of writing www.genealogybank.com had 125 million articles, from more than 500,000 issues of about 2,500 historical U.S. newspapers. These newspapers were originally published between 1690 and 1980.

They also have the texts online for searching 11,700 books prior to the year 1900, and 151,000 reports, as well as other lists and documents spanning the years 1789 to 1980. Their website constantly lists newly-added newspapers and I am impressed with the speed at which more content is being digitized and added to their website.

Other newspaper websites you may wish to investigate are:

http://paperspast.natlib.govt.nz
http://smalltownpapers.com
http://dream.lib.utah.edu/digital/unews/
http://db.lib.washington.edu/press/index.html
http://www.loc.gov/chroniclingamerica/
http://nzdl.sadl.uleth.ca/cgi-bin/library?a=p&p=about
&c=niupepa&l=mi&nw=utf-8
http://www.kb.se/
www.secstate.wa.gov/history/newspapers.aspx
http://nupepa.org/cgi-bin/nupepa?l=en (Hawaii)
http://www.nla.gov.au/anplan/ (Australia)

Some newspapers have their own digitization program or indexing programs, or both underway. Here are a few wide-ranging examples:

The Toronto Star (1894-2002)
http://thestar.pagesofthepast.ca

The Times (London, England) (1785-1985)
www.galegroup.com/Times

The Brooklyn Daily Eagle (1841-1902)
www.brooklynpubliclibrary.org/eagle

The Tundra Times (1962-1977)
http://ttip.tuzzy.org

PERSI - The World's Largest Periodical Index

PERSI, The Periodical Source Index, with more than 1.8 million index entries, is the largest subject index to genealogical and historical periodical articles in the world. It was created by the Allen County Public Library in Fort Wayne, Indiana. This library was originally known as the Fort Wayne Public Library.

It covers more than 5,000 periodicals written in English and French (Canada) since the year 1800, although the articles cover the 1700s to the present.

You can access PERSI at:

http://persi.heritagequestonline.com/hqoweb/library/do/persi

Also, www.ancestry.com has a searchable PERSI index, available by subscription:

http://www.ancestry.com/search/db.aspx?dbid=3165

Introducing the Lost Genealogies

Did you know that there are millions of ancestors in a very specific collection of books that have never been indexed?

Are you aware that many of the libraries and archives you've probably visited in the past actually have these books available? You may not have seen them, however, because they are not in the genealogy collection.

Although researchers may work nearby, comparatively few of them have delved into this other collection of books.

This other collection of books contains invaluable records. Families are recorded generation by generation. Many of these genealogies start around the late 1800s and go as far back in time as 1,000 years ago.

Therefore, I have singled out this overlooked collection of books and I refer to them as the Lost Genealogies. If I were to use the old dictionary meaning of "fabulous," it would really apply here. These genealogies are truly *fabulous*.

The purpose of the next chapter is to reveal these Lost Genealogies and to show you why they are the single most unused source of genealogical data in the world today.

NOTES

[1] Klymasz, R. B. [Robert Bogdan]. — *A classified dictionary of Slavic surname changes in Canada.* — Winnipeg : Ukrainian Free Academy of Sciences, 1961. — 64 p. — (Onomastica ; no. 22). — Added title page in Ukrainian. The surname example cited was chosen at random.

[2] Bogdan, F. [Forwin]. — *Dictionary of Ukrainian surnames in Canada.* — Winnipeg : Onomastic Commission of UVAN : Canadian Institute of Onomastic Sciences, 1974. — 50, 354 p. — (Onomastica ; no. 47). — Title on added t.p.: *Dictionnaire des noms de famille ukrainiens au Canada.* Title on added t.p.: *Slovnyk ukraïns'kykh prizvyshch u Kanadi*

[3] Hande, D'Arcy. — *Changes of name : The Saskatchewan gazette, 1917 to 1950.* — Compiled by D'Arcy Hande, Debbie Moyer, Rae Chamberlain. – Regina: Saskatchewan Genealogical Society, c1993. — [3], iii, [1], 89 p.

[4] Roy, Léon, "The Keeping of Church Registers of Judicial Status in the Province of Québec*", Rapport de L'Archiviste de la Province de Québec pour 1959-1960,* Published by Roch Lefebvre, Imprimeur de Sa Majesté La Reine, English section pages 169ff.

[5] *Yarmouth Nova Scotia Genealogies, Transcribed from the Yarmouth Herald,* by George S. Brown, Published by Genealogical Publishing Company, Inc., Baltimore, Maryland, 1993.

The Lost Genealogies

Heraldry, Coats of Arms, and Crests

Coats of arms and crests originated many centuries ago before the general public could read and write. They were popular throughout Europe, the British Isles (United Kingdom) and Japan.

Knights and soldiers in battle, often wearing suits of armor, with their face helmets closed, did not have a clear view of who was who in the midst of fighting, and a split second hesitation could mean the difference between life and death. Certain garments worn over the armor, and specific symbols emblazoned on their shields were the fastest way to distinguish between one of their own or the enemy. They could recognize color patterns and designs easily, even if they were unable to read or write.

The coats of arms were generally issued by a central legal authority in each country, and were usually reserved for people of noble families and royalty.

In England, for example, even today the *College of Arms* continues to grant arms to those who are deemed worthy. The design involves complicated mixes of symbols, colors and replications of animal furs and metals, all with certain meanings and characteristics.

Today you will see coats of arms for cities, provinces, states and countries and are often part of official seals.

It is important to know, however, that there is generally no such thing as a coat of arms or crest for a surname. Coats of arms were granted to individuals, so having the same surname as someone in the past that had a coat of arms does not mean you are a direct descendant of that person.

Heraldry merchants can be found at fairs, malls, and even on the Internet. They may show you a picture of a coat of arms with your surname below it. Beware of this, unless you know—with genealogical evidence— that you are a direct descendant of the original person to whom such arms were granted. Save your money.

Why then, does legitimate heraldry play such an important part in genealogical research? Applicants for coats of arms had to attach genealogical evidence as documentation, which had to be verified as part of the registration of arms. In some cases the coat of arms came with extensive genealogy—or at the very least a brief family history—that's why it is so important.

Such genealogies will trace the ancestry of European families back into the 1300s and sometimes even earlier than that. It is the most neglected area of genealogical research.

Genealogies attached to coats of arms bridge huge gaps that are missing in written records. These genealogies had to be accepted by the authorities granting arms. The authorities had professional experts who thoroughly examined all genealogical evidence. It was very serious business.

Remember that although these arms were originally for noble families, the genealogies would nevertheless often include people that were not of the nobility themselves, including those who were distantly related in some way. Many of these marvelous genealogies would often encompass time periods where genealogical records were either missing or had been destroyed.

More than 250,000 people were awarded coats of arms in the past. Imagine the genealogies and family histories and the connectivity that would be included among such a large number of people. I daresay that millions of people would fall under one huge genealogical umbrella.

As more heraldic genealogies are discovered, more pieces are added to this global jigsaw puzzle that is truly gigantic in size.

As usual, the pessimists will say most records can never be found, whereas optimists and realists can say truthfully that with each passing year, a virtual torrent of new information is emerging and sometimes it originates from the most unlikely places.

How far it will evolve in years to come is anybody's guess, but it will – without any doubt – continue to grow larger and larger as we move into the future where vast storehouses of information and knowledge will reside at our fingertips.

It is also possible that genetics will be able to be combined with what you know of your family tree, to actually extend your genealogy – by person if not by name – back far enough to connect in with ancestors from centuries ago. Still skeptical? Visit the many websites involved in DNA sampling. Here are just a few of many that may surprise you:

www.smgf.org/index.jspx
www.ybase.org/default.asp

The oldest original books combining heraldry and genealogy were all painstakingly made by hand. In a few cases just one original is made. In other cases, copies were made one by one for a limited number of patrons, libraries or archives.

The Genealogical Research Library has copied many of these handwritten books and once the genealogies are completely indexed, they will make them available. Once again, what was once available only to the privileged few in the past will be available to everyone, at little or no cost.

As these books of heraldry with attached genealogies are assembled together and added to the growing genealogical databases, the skeptics who predicted huge gaps would always remain will be proven wrong once again.

The rest of this chapter contains a few samples of heraldic designs and the genealogies associated with them.

I trust that these images – and copies – are worth thousands of words, so I will let them speak for themselves. These are very real examples of The Lost Genealogies.

ADEL D. RUSS. OSTSEEPROVINZEN.

A. IMMATRIKULIRTER ADEL.

Taf. 93.

ERMES.
Bartholomaeus. 1457.

ERMES.
Lorenz. 1547.

ERMES.
Laurenz. 1552.

ERMES c.1650.

v. ERMES ✠.

v. ESSEN.

n.d.Schwed.Natural: Dipl. v. 18. IX. 1643.
(Estht. Linie.)

Ermes, Herren von.

Der Stammsitz dieses Geschlechts, welches die ver-. schiedensten Schreibarten so z. B. Erms, Ergemess, Ergams, Argemess, Armiss etc. im Namen zeigt, ist nicht, wie die Tradition angibt, das Fürstenthum Halberstadt, obwohl es nicht unmöglich ist, dass der Stammvater des Geschlechts in Livland B a r t h o l o m a e u s, der hier bereits 1434, 1438 und 1457 als Bevollmächtigter der Ritterschaft des Gebiets Wenden zu Walck erscheint, aus einem Zweige stammte, der sich im Halberstädtischen niedergelassen hatte. Das Stammland ist vielmehr das Fürstenthum Calenberg der heutigen Provinz Hannover und der Stammsitz E i m s e n an der Leine zwischen Alfeld und Brüggen. Das Hodenbergsche Calenbergische Urkundenbuch führt Theil V Nr. 6 folgende Mitglieder des Geschlechts von 1181—1215 an:

1181 B u r c h a r d de Eimissen.
1184   „   de Emussim.
1184   „   de Emisseim.
1188   „   de Eimesen.
1188   „   de Heimersen.
1189   „   de Eimesheim et frater ejus Herman de Burnem (Bornum).

1191 B u r c h. de Emessem n o b i l i s.
1192 B u r c h. de Heymessem.
1197 B o r c h a r d v. Eimessem, Vater von J o h. und H a h o l d.
1198 B u r c h. de Eimessem, Vater v. J o h. und H a h o l d u s.
1204 B u r c h. v. Emessem, Domh. in Hildesheim.
1206 B u r c h. de Emeshem, Domh. in Hildesheim.
1213 C o n r. de Ymessem.
1215 F r i e d r i c h von Hermesen, Zeuge einer Mindener Urkunde.

um 1280 A l b e r t von Ermissen, dessen sel. Bruder F r i e d r i c h und des Letzteren Töchter Engele und Cunigunde, in einer Urkunde unter Bischof V o l k w i n v. Minden (1275—1291) — Lippische Regesten I. Anh. Nr. 3.
1265 L u d e r de Emessem, im Lüneburgschen.
1300 L u d e r de Emmessen, im Lüneburgischen.

(Die beiden letztgenannten (1265 und 1300) sind wohl von obigen Hildesheimschen Edelleuten verschieden und haben als Stammsitz Embsen im Lüneburgschen.)

Der obengenannte livländische Stammvater des Geschlechts B a r t h o l o m a e u s hatte 2 Söhne: Bartholomaeus (II.) — A r g e m e s und L a u r e n z (der Aeltere genannt) — E r m y s s — die 1486 auftreten Letzterer hinterliess eine Wittwe N. N. geb. v. Guitsleff, die 1505 Repshof erhielt.

Vielleicht ein dritter Bruder derselben und Sohn des B a r t h o l o m a e s war H a n s E r g e m e s s, dessen Schwiegervater, F r o m h o l d Brincken mit ihm am Montag nach Peter und Paul 1467 von D i e d r i c h v. Brincken, dessen Antheil am Dorfe Kippewer, den Hof zu Lemover und das Dorf Kondess (Ksp. Waimel) und Dorf Linnastwer (Ksp. Kapstewer) kauft. 1468 überträgt genannter F r o m h o l d und seine Frau Else genanntem H a n s Ergemess dies erkaufte Gut (Hof Kyppegerwe-Kibbijerw i/E.) dem der D. O. M. Berend v. d. Borch dasselbe d. d. Wenden 1474 Dienstag nach Michaelis bestätigt.

Er war 1505 todt; seine Söhne R e i n h o l d u. L o r e n z II., (der junge genannt) erhalten d. d. 26. Mai 1505 K i b b i j e r w und den Besitz v. Repshof (s. oben Laurenz) durch den Comthnr von Fellin: W e n n e m a r v. Delwig zugesprochen.

R e i n h o l d, der schon 1501 urkundlich, ist wohl erblos verstorben, wogegen L o r e n z II. die genannten Güter, wie auch Schloss Lude (das einer seiner Söhne J o h a n n indess 9. September 1518 dem J o h a n n von Plettenberg auftrug) übernahm.

Ausser J o h a n n hatte L o r e n z II. noch 3 Söhne: I.) L o r e n z III. (todt 1539) dessen Wittwe 1539 Pfandbesitzerin von Kondes war und dessen Sohn L o r e n z IV. 1541 Mandever und Moisema i/E. verpfändete. 1547 und 1549. 1554 1559 urkundlich auf Kojel und Sall i/E. erscheint und erblos am 11. September 1560 gegen die Russen im Gefecht blieb, II) R e i n h o l d und III) F r o m hold.

Diese beiden theilten am 11. Juni 1549 das ihnen von ihrem Stiefvater J o h a n n v. Wrangel auf Luhde als Entschädigung für gewisse Ansprüche eine Zeitlang entzogen gewesene, aber vom Comthur zu Fellin am 26. Mai 1540 wieder zugesprochene Dorf Kiblijerw (s. oben) wozu damals der gleichnamige Hof, die Dörfer Lemmofer, Kowtts, Toylemets, die Mühle zu Watsilli, das Gesinde an der Arro und der Krug zu Wemel, wie das Dorf Atzejerwe (Ahtjerwe), das sie 1552 verkaufen, gehörte.

Ende des 16. Jahrhunderts besassen die Gebrüder Lorenz und Jacob (beide todt 1600) Kiblijerw, sowie die (von Lorenz IV. ererbten) Güter Sall und Ottenküll i/L. Ihre Kinder erhielten vom Herzog Carl von Südermanland am 5. Dezember 1600 Kibbijerw bestätigt, was Kunigunde, Tochter oder Enkelin, eines von ihnen nebst Sall und Ottenküll ihrem Gemahl Heinrich v. Stryk 1632 zubrachte.

Vorher schon, nämlich am 22. März 1597 d. d. Warschau bestätigte K. Sigmund III. von Polen einem Caspar I. v. Ermes die Güter Kokenberg und Wiegandshof (auch Ermeshof) geheissen, die schon (wahrscheinlich) Hans zur Ordenszeit besessen hatte, als alte Erbgüter. Dieselben vererbten auf Caspars I. Sohn: Caspar II., dem sie, als Schwed. Regimentsquartiermeister, er starb vor 1649 als Oberst und Commandant v. Erfurt) v. Schweden bestätigt wurden. Seinen unmündigen Kindern (aus der Ehe mit Anna v. Löwenwolde) (geb. 1609 † 1648) wurde von der Königin Christine am 6. Juli 1649 die nochmalige Bestätigung darüber zu Theil. Von diesen Kindern hinterliess anscheinend nur Johann Caspar († vor 1682 als schwed. Rittmeister) Nachkommen, denen die Schwed. Reductionskommission am 23. Januar 1683 die Güter ebenfalls beliess, desgleichen Pnikeln, was der Familie aus Tiesenhausenschen Besitz vererbt war.

In die Livländische Adelsmatrikel wurde (in die Matrikeln v. 1742, 1745 und 1747) die Familie v. E. bei Klasse I sub Nr. 1 verzeichnet und zwar die Häuser Kokenberg und Wiegandshof, welche damals Johann Arend v. B., 1743 Ordnungsgerichtsadjunkt, dann Ordnungsrichter besass, der sie 1749, nebst Puikeln, verkaufte und der auch Jummerdehn inne hatte, was die Erben des Kammerjunkers v. E. 1784 verkauften.

Eine derselben (wohl die Letzte ihres Geschlechts) war Wilhelmine v. E., welche sich mit dem Hofrath v. Berg auf Mahlenhof vermählte und eines Ahnin ist des Feldmarschalls Grafen v. Berg, der auch ihr Wappen in das seinige aufgenommen hat. In Esthland ist die Familie am 8. Februar 1745 als notorisch bei Klasse I (Nr. 22) eingetragen, aber dort bald ebenfalls erloschen.

Wappen.
(Tafel 93.)

Das zuletzt, allerdings auch mit vielen Varianten in Farbe und Stellung, geführte Wappen war ein getheilter Schild, in dessen oberem silbernen Felde 2 gekrönte Mohrenrümpfe in schwarzen goldverbrämten Röcken, mit Armstummeln, von bzw. schräglinkem und schrägrechtem goldenem (alias grünem) Pfeile in die äussere Hüfte geschossen, aus dem unteren Felde, worin ein goldschwarzes Schach, wachsen. Auf dem gekrönten Helme mit schwarzgoldsilbernen Decken der rechte Mohrenrumpf.

Die auf Tafel 93 nach dem Siegel des Laurenz Ermes (Arrimis) v. 1552 gezeichneten Wappen hat statt der Mohrenrümpfe einen halben Moskowiter u. dgl. Königin.

Das älteste bekannte Siegel (des Bartholomaeus v. E., v. J. 1457) zeigt unter 2 am Halse abgeschnittenen Mannsköpfen im Schildhaupte, 9 (3. 3. 3) Pfennige im Schilde; dagegen führt Lorenz Ermes 1547 einen ganz dem Wappen, der „von Dücker" ähnelnden Wappen schild (mehrere Balken oder Schach).

Das spätere Wappen c. 1650 war:

Schild: quergetheilt durch schmalen rothen Balken, oben in Silber wachsend 2 gekrönte Jünglingsrümpfe, vorwärtsgekehrt, mit Armstummeln, silbernem Rock und schwarzem Mäntelchen, je senkrecht durchbohrt von gestürztem Schwert; unten von Schwarz und Gold in 4 Reihen geschacht.

Helm (gekrönt): wachsend ein desgleichen Rumpf.

Decken: rothgolden-schwarzsilbern.

Das jetzige Wappen. Der rechte Rumpf mit blauem Rock und goldenen Mäntelchen, der linke umgekehrt.

Helm (gekrönt): mit wachsendem blaugekleidetem Mann, der ein goldenes Linienzepter hält.

Decken: blaugolden-schwarzgolden.

ABGESTORB. PREUSS. ADEL.

PROVINZ SCHLESIEN.

Taf. 50.

MEDIGER, III.

MEHL v. STRELITZ, I.

MEHL v. STRELITZ, II.

MELTZER gen. ESCHLAUER.

MELZER v. FRIEDBERG, adl. W.

MELZER v. FRIEDBERG, Fhrn.

METTICH, St. W.

METTICH, St. W.

METTICH, St. W.

METTICH, Fhrn.

METTICH, Gfn.

MEYWALDT.

Mettich (Grafen v. M., Freiherrn von Tschetschau).
(Taf. 50.)

Böhmischer Freiherrenstand dto. 1605. 9. 9. für Joachim v. M. und seine Vettern Balthasar, Hans und Georg; Reichsgrafenstand dto. 1633. 12. 11. für Joachim Frhrn. v M.

Uraltes schlesisches Geschlecht, welches seit Beginn des XIV. Jahrhunderts in schlesischen und glätzischen Urkunden unter dem Namen Czeczow, Czechow, Czeschow vorkommt; der Name Mettich wurde von dem Gute Mettkau (Mettichow, Metchow, Medgow) wohl angenommen. In glätzischen Urkunden erscheinen 1316 Otto und Tamme (Thomas) Cz., 1412 Hans Cz. und noch 1456 ein anderer Hans Cz. Als Stammvater des Geschlechtes dürfte Schibko oder Schibeschin v. Cz. zu Gross-Peterwitz und Polsnitz (Kr. Neumarkt) zu betrachten sein, welcher mit Herzog Bernhard von Münsterberg in der Schlacht bei Mühldorf kämpfte und bis 1360 erwähnt wird. Dessen Nachkommen Thamme, Otto und Friedrich werden unter dem Namen „Medgow zu Ossig" (Kr. Striegau) erwähnt, wogegen Kuno 1391 als „Metschow" aufgeführt wird. Des letzteren Nachkommen Scheijbechin, Hans und Fredemann „Metchow" verkaufen 1405 Polsnitz an das Vinzenzstift in Breslau; Georg v. „Metchaw" 1452 auf Ingramsdorf (Kr. Schweidnitz); 1454 Heinrich v. „Tzetschaw", Erbherr auf Paulsdorf (Pohlsdorf, Kr. Neumarkt). Von letzterem stammte Hans auf „Metche" (Mettkau, Kr. Neumarkt) und Borganie (ibid.), welcher als der nähere Stammvater der Freiherren und Grafen von Mettich zu betrachten ist und 1496 starb. Er hinterliess 3 Söhne: Balthasar auf „Metche" 1502—1540, Kaspar auf Borganie († 1553) und Hans auf Neudorf (Kr. Neumarkt) † 1551. Kaspars Nachkommenschaft erlosch mit seinen Enkeln; von Balthasar stammte Ladislaus, Amtmann der Commende Gröbnig, welcher um 1570 Zeiselwitz (Kr Neustadt), sowie 1584 Mochau (ibid.) und Gläsen (Kr. Leobschütz) erwarb († 1585); von Hans stammten Christoph und Nicolaus (welche 1569 Hilbersdorf bei Falkenberg erkauften), Joachim (welcher 1607 das Seniorat Wiese mit den Gütern Langenbrück, Riegersdorf, Buchelsdorf,

Dittmannsdorf etc im Kreise Neustadt stiftete) und
Caspar (bis 1597 auf Hünern, seit 1602 auf Schräbsdorf
c. pert.). Die Söhne Ladislaus: Balthasar, Hans und
Georg, sowie Nicolaus Sohn Joachim wurden in den Freiherrenstand erhoben; letzterer später auch in den Grafen-
stand. Dieselben übernahmen 1604 die Schlossherrschaft
Ratibor in Pfandbesitz, welche 1609 in Erbbesitz über-
ging und bis 1631 bei dem Geschlechte blieb. Balthasar
(† 1612 oder 1613) hinterliess von seiner Gemahlin Helena v. Schaffgotsch zwei Töchter und einen Sohn, Hans
Christoph, welcher nach kinderloser Ehe mit Juliana v.
Zvole und Goldstein 1635 starb; Hans war 1579 Comthur des Johanniterordens zu Klein-Oels, 1585 zu Lossen
und Gross-Tinz und starb 1610 als k. k. Kämmerer, Hof-
Kammerrath und Ober-Silberkämmerer; Georg hinterliess
bei seinem Tode 1613 aus seiner Ehe mit Maria v. Bauch
einen Sohn, Hans Georg, mit welchem seine Nachkommenschaft erlosch. Joachim setzte den Stamm dauernd
fort, bis derselbe mit dem Tode des Grafen Heinrich Josef
Ferdinand 1853. 11. 4. im Mannesstamme erlosch.

Aus der adligen Linie (von Kaspar abstammend) war
Hans auf Wiersbel (Kr. Falkenberg) und Schräbsdorf k.
k. Rath und Hauptmann von Münsterberg und Franken-
stein († 1621) und dessen Bruder Nicolaus († zw. 1614
—18) Johanniterordens Comthur zu Klein-Oels (seit 1609),
erzherzoglicher Kämmerer und Geh. Rath; mit des erste-
ren Söhnen aus der Ehe mit Anna Maria v. Zedlitz —
Hans Nicolaus auf Schräbsdorf († 1625) und Karl — erlosch dieser Zweig. Ausserdem blühte noch — von oben-
genanntem Georg (1452) abstammend — eine adlige Linie, in deren Besitz Gregersdorf, Paulsdorf (Pohlsdorf),
Ingramsdorf, Roth-Kirschdorf, Schmachtenhayn, Struse,
Seifersdorf, Mittel-Peilau, Langen-Neudorf, Guhrwitz,
Karisch etc. erscheinen; doch erlosch auch diese Linie
in der zweiten Hälfte des XVII. Jahrhunderts.

Die sichere Stammreihe des Geschlechtes ist folgende: 1) Hans auf Metche und Borganie († 1496); Gem.
Margaretha Stolz von Schlanz (bis 1517): — 2) Hans
auf Neudorf und Hünern († 1551. 19. 6.); Gem. I. Hed-
wig v. d. Heyde a. d H. Lauterbach († 1539); II. Anna
v. Biedau († 1567); — 3) Nicolaus von Hünern zu Weig-
witz, Schönborn und Antheil Rosenau († c. 1589); Gem.

Helena v. Haase zu Klein-Rädlitz († 1618); — 4) Joachim (Freiherr 1605, Graf 1633), k. k. wirkl. Geh. Rath und Kämmerer, Ober-Silberkämmerer, königl. poln. und schwed. Rath, seit 1645 Landeshauptmann der Fürstenthümer Oppeln und Ratibor (* 1578, † 1616. 23. 9.); Gem. I. 1610 ?; II 1626 Anna Maria Gräfin Dohna zu Wartenberg; — 5) Karl Joachim (* 1627, † 1684. 14. 9.); Gem. Anna Maria Freiin Proskowsky von Proskau; — 6) Karl Christoph (* 1655. 30. 11., † 1703); Gem. 1687 Maria Sabina Gräfin v. Verdugo (* 1658. 29. 3., † 1712. 30. 4.); — 7) Karl Joachim (* 1693. 31. 5., † 1748. 15. 10.); Gem. Maria Johanna Freiin v. Welczeck (* 1704. 12. 2., † 1767. 13. 4); — 8) Franz Karl Johann Anton Josef, k. k. Kämmerer und Oberst (* 1737. 7. 6., † 1819. 21. 6.); Gem. I. 1768. 21. 11. Maria Johanna Gräfin Althann (* 1743. 18. 9., † 1784. 17. 1.); II. 1787. 26. 7. Josefa Maria Gräfin Althann (* 1752. 18 5., † 1807. 6. 5.); 9) Heinrich Josef Ferdinand (* 1778. 13. 9., † 1853. 11. 4.); Gem. 1803. 13 9. Maria Anna Freiin von Saurma-Jeltsch (* 1786. 7. 1., † 1836. 5. 4.); letzterer adoptirte seiner Schwester Tochter Karolina Anna Franciska Agnes Mohr v. Ehrenfeld (* 1815. 11. 6., † 1865. 31. 5.), welche sich in zweiter Ehe 1859. 11. 6. mit Rudolf Maria Bernhard Grafen v. Stillfried-Rattonitz und Neurode, Granden von Portugal und Grafen von Alcántara. kön. preuss. wirkl. Geh. Rath und Ober-Ceremonienmeister vermählte.

Die Reihe der Senioratsherren auf Wiese ist nachstehende: I. Joachim (* 1537, † 1612); — II. Joachim (vid. oben Nr. 4); — III. Wolf Nicolaus († 1655. 29. 6.), k. k. Kämmerer und Schlosshauptmann zu Ratibor; — IV. Karl Joachim (vid. oben Nr. 5); — V. Johann Joachim († 1697. 6. 10.); Gem. Johanna Theresia Gräfin v. Herberstein (verm. 1673 28. 11.); — VI. Johann Leopold († 1703. 18. 5.); Gem. Euphemia Eleonora Gräfin Althann (* 1668. 11. 6., † nach 1710); — VII. Ferdinand Maximilian (* 1688, † 1743. 9. 6.), Landrechtsbeisitzer der Fürstenthümer Oppeln und Ratibor und Landeshauptmann derselben Fürstenthümer; Gem. 1714. 22. 7. Maria Johanna Gräfin v. Schrattenbach (* 1692, † 1745. 25. 5); — VIII. Karl Joachim (vid. oben Nr. 7); —

IX. Karl Christoph Josef Jacob Heinrich (* 1723. 25. 7;
† 1780. 17 6.); Gem. 1751. 18. 7. Maria Anna Franziska
Freiin v. Gruttschreiber (* 1722. 4. 11., † 1786. 4. 6.);
— X. Franz Karl Johann Anton Josef (vid. oben Nr. 8);
— XI. Karl Magnus Johann Nepomuk (* 1774. 23. 3.,
† 1825. 20. 8.), Landesältester des Kreises Neustadt O|S.;
Gem. I. 1795. 15. 11. Maria Antonia Gräfin v. Karwath
(* 1772. 9. 1., † 1805. 12. 8.); II. 1806. 13. 4. Maria
Anna Gräfin Henckel v. Donnersmarck (* 1775. 8. 6.,
† 1829. 28. 5.). Nach dem Tode des Gfen Karl Magnus
kam die Senioratsherrschaft mit Genehmigung der Agna-
ten zum Verkauf.

Das Geschlecht ist gänzlich 1886 erloschen mit der
Gräfin Maria Antonia Josefa (* 1806. 13. 10.), verm.
1835. 20. 10. mit Josef Grafen von Larisch, Freiherrn von
Ellguth und Karwin (* 1777. 3. 12., † 1841. 3. 12.), k. k.
Kämmerer und k. preuss. Generalmajor a. D.

Die nachstehend aufgeführte 64feldige Ahnentafel der
Gräfin Maria Antonia gibt einen Beweis für die weit aus-
gedehnte Verwandtschaft des Mettichschen Geschlechtes
und enthält folgende Geschlechter. 1) Graf von Mettich,
Freiherr von Tschetschau; — 2) Burggraf von Dohna;
— 3) Freiherr Proskowsky von Proskau; — 4) Freiherr
Kochtizky von Kochtitz; — 5) Graf von Verdugo; —
6) Freiherr Zajic von Hasenburg; — 7) Freiherr Lieb-
steinský von Kolovrat; — 8) Freiherr Colonna von Fels;
9) Freiherr von Welczek und Gross-Dubensko; —
10) ?; — 11) Graf von Praschma, Freiherr von Bilkau;
— 12) von Gusnar und Komorno; — 13) Freiherr von
Berchtoldt und Ungarschitz; — 14) Freiherr Hegenmüller
von Dubenweiler; — 15) Graf von Sprinzenstein; —

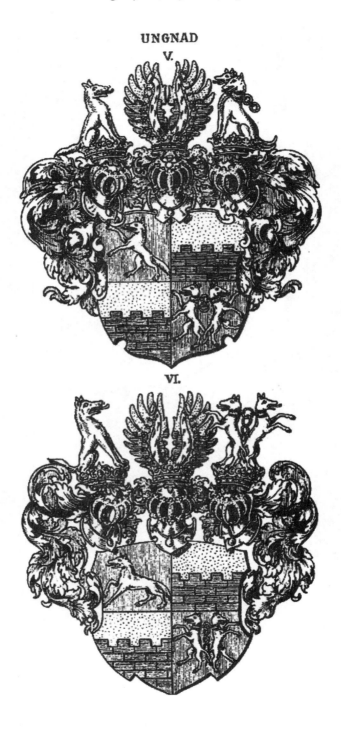

Ungnad v. Weissenwolff.
(Tafel 206, 207).

W: I. (Siegel 1295): Ein rechtschreitender Wolf. Der Helm trägt einen off. Flug. — II. (Wiener Minoriten Necrologium 1340): In R. ein rechtsspringender aufgerichteter s. Wolf mit niedergekehrtem Wedel. — III. (Steirisches Wappenbuch des Joh. Gottfried Hertzenkrafft aus dem Ende des 16. Jhdts): Wie vorhin, aber der Wolf linksgewendet. Der gekr. Helm mit r.-s. Decke trägt den Wolf wachsend. — IV. (1449): Geviert; 1 u. 4 wie II, 2 u. 3 in G. eine vier Quadersteine hohe schwarz ausgefugte dreimal gezinnte bl. Mauer (Dumersdorf). Zwei gekr. Helme. Der rechte mit r.-s. Decke trägt den Wolf auf die Hinterläufe niedergetan, der linke mit bl.-g. Decke zwei Büffelshörner, das rechte s., das linke r., jedes aussen mit einem gezahnten g. Kamme besetzt. — V. (1456): Geviert; 1, 2 u. 3 wie vorhin, 4 in R. zwei springende, mit den Köpfen voneinander, mit den Rücken gegeneinandergekehrte aufgerichtete, mit einer an ihren g. Halsbändern befestigten g. Kette zusammengekoppelte s. Rüden mit aufgereckten Ohren u. schräggekreuzt verschlungenen Schwänzen (Plankenwart). Drei gekr. Helme. Der rechte wie bei IV, der mittl. mit bl.-g. Decke trägt vor einem off. wie Feld 2 bezeichneten Adlersfluge zwei mit Hermelin überzogene Büffelshörner, jedes aussen mit einem g. Kamme besetzt, welcher an seinen sieben Zacken mit aus g. Knöpfen hervorgehenden Hahnenfedern besteckt ist u. der linke Helm mit r.-s. Decke trägt die beiden Rüden mit rückwärts abhängender Kette nebeneinander auf die Hinterläufe niedergetan. — VI. (Steiermärk. Wappenbuch des Zacharias Bartsch vom Jahre 1567): Wie vorhin, aber der Wolf im 1. Felde rechtsschreitend u. die Mauer im 2. u. 3. Felde mit 4 Zinnen, deren äussere in den Feldesrand treten. Der linke Helm trägt die beiden Rüden wie im 4. Felde.

Kärtner Uradel.

I. Otto Ungnad, † nach 17. I. 1201, ⚰ Stift St. Paul. — II. Otto Ungnad, † nach 5. IV. 1236. — III.

1) Wolfram, bischöfl. Bamberg. Schenk, † nach 4. IV. 1241. — 2) Heinrich Ungnad, † nach 13. X. 1245, ✕ I) mit Gertrud v. Mernburg; II) mit Kyburg v. Ehrenfels. — 3) Otto, † nach 3. III. 1246. — IV. Otto Ungnad, 1275, ✕ mit einer v. Lippowitz. Söhne: 1. Konrad, 1278. — 2. Otto der Aelt., w. f. — 3. Ulrich Ungnad, 1282—1287. Söhne: 1) Bernhard, Rr, 1323. — 2) Ulrich Ungnad, Rr 1323, ✕ mit Demut, T. d. Johann v. Kuchlau v. Hohenkuchel. Tochter: Anna, ✕ mit Heinrich Burggfen zu Görz.

V. Otto Ungnad der Aelt. auf Waldenstein u. Limberg, Rr, † nach 28. VIII. 1305, ✕ mit Barbara, T. d. Otto v. Zinzendorf. Kinder: 1) Katharina, ✕ vor 19. VI. 1303 mit Otto dem Jüng. v. Weissenegg, 1308. — 2) Friedrich, Domherr zu Salzburg, † nach 31. III. 1312. — 3) Otto der Jüng., † nach 3. V. 1325, ✕ I) vor 9. V. 1319 mit . . . . ., T. d. Friedrich Sachs; II) vor 24. IV. 1332 mit Elisabeth, T. d. Otto des Aelt. v. Traun auf Hauseck u. d. Anna v. Zinzendorf. — 4) Konrad, † Wien IX. Kal. Dec. 1340, ⚰ bei den Minoriten, ✕ mit Gertraud Graland a. d. H. Leonburg, † nach 21. XII 1348. — 5) Wolfgang, w. f.

VI. Wolfgang Ungnad auf Waldenstein u. Wasserleonburg, bischöfl. Bamberg. Burggraf zu Wolfsberg, † nach 23. VIII. 1358, ✕ vor 16. IX. 1346 mit Anna, T. d. Wolfhart v. Hanau, 1367. Kinder: (1) Wolfhart, w. f. — (2) Anna, 1388, ✕ mit Wilhelm dem Jüng. v. Schärffenberg auf Ruckenstein, † 1398. — (3) Otto Ungnad auf Waldenstein, Rr, † nach 6. I. 1388, ✕ mit Wandula v. Gradenegg. Kinder: 1. Barbara, ✕ 1392 mitKonrad Frut dem Jüng. auf Plankenwart. — 2. Martha, † 1434, ⚰ St. Johanneskapelle Duino, 1388 ✕ mit Johann v. Reichenburg. — 3. Pankraz, hzgl. Pfleger zu Bleiburg, † 1441 Samstag nach Maximilian, ⚰ Pfarrkirche Graz, ✕ I) 1419 mit Agnes, T. d. Johann Markgfen v. Hochberg u. d. Agnes v. Geroldseck, † 2. II. 1425 (war ✕ in 1. Ehe mit Friedrich Gfen v. Ortenburg, † 29. V. 1418); II) 1435 mit Margareta, T. d. Dietegen Truchsess v. Emmerberg auf Halbenrain,† als Wwe, Sohn: Andreas, + Wien 1424. ⚰ bei St. Stefan.

VII. **Wolfhart Ungnad, Rr,** † nach 13. IV. 1385,
✕ mit **Johanna Schenk v. Osterwitz,** ⚰ Minoriten-
kloster Wolfsberg. Kinder: 1. **Konrad Ungnad,** bischöfl.
Bamberg. Burggraf zu Griffen, † zwischen Georgi 1405
u. 1420, ✕ I) mit **Anna,** T. d. Heinrich v. Rappach
auf Klamm u. Pitten u. d. Katharina v. Rottenmann;
II) mit **Wandula,** T. d. Thomas Gfen v. St. Georgen u.
Bösing. Torhter: **Demuth,** ✕ mit Heinrich Graland
auf Leonburg. — 2. **Ursula,** † als Wwe, ✕ mit Burk-
hard v. Rabenstein auf Sonnegg, † vor 20. VI. 1425.
— 3. **Luzia,** ✕ 1420 mit Ulrich v. Weissbriach. —
4. **Wolfgang,** w. f.

VIII. **Wolfgang Ungnad auf Heunburg,** bischöfl.
Bamberg. Burggraf zu Griffen, † zwischen Mittwoch vor
St. Ruprecht 1428 u. Freitag vor Sonntag Invocavit in
der Fasten 1429, ✕ 1402 mit **Margareta,** T. d. Berenger
Dumersdorfer u. d. . . . . . v. Plankenwart, † nach 17.
XI. 1443. Kinder: 1) **Johann Ungnad auf Waldenstein,**
Gradenegg, Liebenberg, Halbenrain, Dietrichstein, Feld-
kirchen, Wiederdriess, Sonnegg u. Plankenwart, kais.
Rat u. Kammermeister, in den n.-ö. Hstd aufgen.
1451, erhielt Mittwoch vor Georgi 1449 u. s. d. Wiener
Neustadt Samstag vor St. Peterstag 1456 Wappenbesse-
rungen, † Wiener Neustadt 1461, ⚰ Pfarrkirche Graz,
✕ 1437 mit **Richarda v. Pernegg.** Tochter: **Anna,**
kais. Hofdame, † Abend vor Martini 1460, ✕ Wiener
Neustadt Ostern 1454 mit Michael R.Burggfen v. Mag-
deburg Gfen zu Hardegg auf Pulkau, Weitersfeld,
Haugsdorf, Markersdorf, Waltersdorf, Pleissing, Raschbach,
Marchegg, Retz, Ober- u. Unter-Nalb, Höflein, Röschitz,
Zellerndorf, Schrems, Therasburg, Mallebern, Reikers-
dorf, Pernsdorf, Hatzendorf, Schönfeld, Alberndorf, Pfaf-
fendorf, Neu-Ruppersdorf, Leodagger, Staatz, Pirach,
Mitterberg, Werfenstein, Freyenstein, Weissenberg u.
Velben, † Wien 24, III. 1483, ⚰ Chor der Augustiner-
kirche. — 2) **Wolfgang, Rr,** † unverm. Rom zwischen 4.
VII. 1452 u. Juli 1456. — 3) **Georg,** kais. Rat u. Hptm.
zu Ortenburg, † unverm. St. Agnestag 1468, ⚰ Kirche
Eberndorf. — 4) **Otto,** † zwischen 1. IX. 1447 u. April
1449, ⚰ Ofen. — 5) **Christof,** w. f. — 6) **Margareta,**
✕ mit Johann v. Schönberg. — 7. **Elisabeth,** ✕ mit
Leonhard Schenk v. Osterwitz.

IX. Christof Ungnad, s. d. Wiener Neustadt
vor dem Palmtag 1463 Panierherr v. Sonnegg
auf Waldenstein, Gradenegg, Liebenberg, Halbenrain,
Dietrichstein, Feldkirchen, Stein, Plankenwart u. Wasserleonburg, kais. Rat u. Hptm. zu Cilli, erhielt Mittwoch
vor Georgi 1449 u. s. d. Wiener Neustadt Samstag vor
St. Peterstag 1456 Wappenbesserungen, wurde 1451 in
den n.-ö. Hstd aufgen., † Donnerstag nach Dreikö-
nigstag 1490, ☖ Pfarrkirche Eberndorf, ✕ 1462 mit
Anna Katharrna, T. d. Rrs Johann des Jüng. v. Fraun-
berg auf Haag u. Mässenhausen u. d. Anna Marschall
v. Pappenheim, † nach 1472. Kinder: (1) Johann, w. f.
— (2) Katharina, ✕ I) mit Andreas v. Hohenwart auf
Gerlachstein u. Krupp, † 1505; II) mit Johann Joachim
v. Purgstall auf Selzach, Rr, 1517. — (3) Maria, ✕
1505 mit Wiguleus vom Thurn auf Neubeuern, † 1540,
beide ☖ St. Jakobskapelle Salzburg.

X. Johann Ungnad, Panierherr v. Sonnegg auf Waldenstein, Gradenegg, Liebenberg, Halbenrain, Dietrichstein, Feldkirchen, Stein, Plankenwart u. Wasserleonburg, † Griffen vor 1520, ✕ mit Margareta, T. d. Leonhard Lochner v. Liebenfels u. d. . . . . . v. Wildenstein.
Kinder: 1. Johann, w. f. s. u. Aelt. Linie. — 2. Andreas, w. f. s. u. Jüng. Linie. — 3. Christof, † 1522
nach Montag vor Georgi. — 4. Polyxena, † 1578, ✕
mit Peter Laso v. Castilien, beide ☖ Augustinerhof-
kirche Wien. — 5. Elisabeth, † 1575, ✕ mit Albrecht
Schlik RGfen zu Bassano auf Budenitz, Bürglitz, El-
bogen, Fünfhunden, Kaaden, Königsberg, Kruschowitz,
Srbeč, Winteritz, Wohnung u. Zlonitz, † 1556. — 6.
Barbara, ehzgl. Hofdame, † nach 6. III. 1563, ✕ Inns-
bruck 1523 mit Wilhelm v. Puchheim auf Heidenreich-
stein u. Gmünd, † 1542.

Aeltere Linie: Sonnegg (erloschen).

XI. Johann Ungnad, s. d. Brüssel 29. V. 1522
RFrbr zu Sonnegg auf Waldenstein, Wasserleonburg,
Ring, Gottschee, Pack, Modriach u. Hirschegg, kgl. Rat
u. Obster Stallmeister u. Vorschneider, s. d. Prag 1.
XII. 1543 Erbobergespan des Warasdiner Komitats, Ober-
ster Feldhptm. in Kroatien u. an der windischen Grenze,

Ldeshptm. in Steiermark bis 1556, seit 1552 Landstand in Krain, * in Steiermark 1486, † auf Winteritz 27. XII. 1564, ⚰ Fürstengruft der Kirche Tü-
bingen, ╳ I) mit Anna Maria, Erbt. d. Georg v. Thurn
auf Friedrichstein, Gurkfeld u. Klingenfeld u. d. Helena
Frangipani a. d. H. Veglia; II) auf Barby 1. VII. 1555
mit Maria Magdalena, T. d. Wolfgang RGfen zu
Barby, Mühlingen, Rosenburg u. Walternienburg u. d.
Agnes RGfin zu Mansfeld a. d. H. Seeburg, * 1530, †
Wien 16. XI. 1565, ⚰ neben ihrem Gemal. Kinder: a) aus
1. Ehe: 1)Ludwig, kais. Km., Rat, Hptm. u. Vizedom zu
Cilli, † Klagenfurt nach 1. VIII. 1586, ⚰ Stadtpfarr-
kirche das., ╳ 8. X. 1581 mit Anna Maria, Erbt. d.
Wilhelm Neumann auf Wasserleonburg, Treffen, Leon-
stein u. Döllach u. d. Barbara Rumpf a. d. H. Wüllross,
* Villach 23. XI. 1535, † auf Murau 18. XII. 1623, ⚰
Spitalskirche das. (war ╳ in 1. Ehe im Oktbr 1557 mit
Johanna Jakob RFrhrn v. Thannhausen, † Friesach
23. IX. 1560, ⚰ Dominikanerkirche das. u. in 2. Ehe
10. I. 1565 mit Christof v. Liechtenstein, † 1580, u.
wieder ╳ in 4. Ehe 9. II. 1587 mit Karl Frhrn v.
Teuffenbach auf Offenburg, † auf Stattenberz zwi-
schen 12. I. u. 6. IX. 1610, in 5. Ehe auf Murau 13.
XI. 1611 mit Ferdinand v. Salamanca RGfen zu Ortenburg Frhen zu Freienstein, Karlsbach, Lill u. Eri-
court auf Oberfalkenstein, † Klagenfurt 1616 u. in 6.
Ehe 1617 mit Georg Ludwig RGfen zu Schwarzenberg
u. Hohenlandsberg auf Haag u. Elsbethenzell, † auf
Freudenau 22. VII. 1646, ⚰ Kapuzinerkloster Murau).
— 2) Christof Ungnad RFrhr zu Sonnegg auf Szamobor
Erbobergespan des Warasdiner Komitats, kais. Rat,
Oberst u. Kmdt zu Erlau, Banus in Kroatien u. Dalma-
tien, † Kaschau im Dezbr 1585, ╳ mit Anna Katharina, T. d. Stefan Lossonczy de genere Tomaj u. d.
Anna Pekry v. Petrovina, † Szomolány (war wieder ╳
in 2. Ehe mit Nikolaus Báthori v. Ecsed, † 1585, u.
in 3. Ehe mit Siegmund Forgách v. Ghymes auf Ta-
polcsány, Szecsöd, Szamos, Keö, Szaláncz u. Szent-Már-
ton, † Tyrnau 23. VI. 1621). Tochter: Anna Maria,
* 1569, † 1611, ╳ Pressburg 29. I. 1584 mit Thomas
Gfen Erdödy v. Monyorókerék u. Monoszló auf Ehrau,
† auf Krapina 17. I. 1624, ⚰ Kirche Agram. — 3) Si-

meon Ungnad RFrhr zu Sonnegg auf Waldenstein, Himmelstein, Höll, Kleingrün, Endersgrün, Mühlendorf,
Wotsch, Bocksgrün u. Weigersdorf, kais. Hptm., hzgl.
sächs. Kmhr, † Gersdorf in Thüringen zwischen 14. IV.
1603 u. Mai 1607, ✕ Saalfeld 1571 mit Katharina,
Erbt. d. Dietrich Edl. Herrn v. Plesse u. d. Katharina
Reuss v. Plauen a. d. H. Greiz (war ✕ in 1. Ehe mit
Johann RGfen zu Gleichen-Blankenheim auf Rhembda,
† 1567). Tochter: Anna Maria Sofia, * Sonntag Qua-
simodogeniti 1573, tot 1612, ✕ 7. IX. 1601 mit Christof RGfen zu Leiningen-Westerburg auf Schaum-
burg, † 1632. — 4) Karl, † unverm. Gastein 1599, ⚰
Völkermarkt. — 5) Ehrenreich, † das. 1598, ✕ mit
..... Peuscher v. Leonstein (war ✕ in 1. Ehe mit
Karl v. Liechtenstein auf Murau, † zwischen 1572 u.
1574). — 7) Judith Elisabeth, † 8. III. 1572, ✕
Wien 1548 mit Johann Baptist dem Jüng. Gfen Hoyos
Frhrn zu Stüchsenstein auf Tribuswinkel, † 27. X. 1568.
— 7) Anna Maria, ✕ 1552 mit Jaroslaw dem Jüng.
v. Kolowrat-Liebsteinský auf Petersburg u. Rabenstein, † 1595. — 8) Felizitas Margareta Maria, † 18.
III. 1570, ✕ mit Pankraz v. Windisch-Graetz
RFrhrn zu Waldstein [u. im Thal, † 29. X. 1591. — b)
aus 2. Ehe: 9) Johann Georg, † unverm. Venedig 25. V.
583. — 10) Wolfgang, † 38 Jahre alt unverm. Sauer-
brunn bei Cilli 1594, ⚰ Völkermarkt.

Jüngere Linie: Bleiburg.

XI. Andreas Ungnad, s. d. Brüssel 29. V. 1532
RFrhr zu Sonnegg auf Dietrichstein, Plankenwart,
Wasserleonburg u. Zwikowetz, seit 1552 Landstand
in Krain, kais. Rat u. Oberststallmeister, † auf Sonnegg 1557, ⚰ Kirche Bleiburg, ✕ I) 1525 mit Anna
Apollonia Maria, T. d. Johann Lang v. Wellenburg u.
d. Maria Margareta Sultzer, Wwe des Christof Julius
Gfen v. Lodron; II) Samstag nach St. Franz 1534
mit Johanna Benigna, Erbt. d. Adalbert v. Pernstein
auf Frauenberg u. Hradištko u. d. Johanna v. Wartenberg; III) 1551 mit Anna, T. d. Johann Hofmann
Frhrn zu Grünpüchel u. Strechau auf Offenburg, Gross-

Sölk, Wolkenstein, Stainach, Schrattenberg, Radkersburg,
Ganowitz, Tüffer, Kaisersberg, Cammern, Mautern, Spiel-
berg a. d. Donau, Wildenstein, Kammer, Kogel, Franken-
burg, Neu-Attersee, Rannariedl, Steyr, Molle, Kremsdorf,
Wels, Gleiss, Garsch, Senftenberg, Oberwallsee, Alt- u.
Neu-Lembach, Seldenhofen, Wartenstein, Bruck a. d.
Leitha, Neukirchen u. Aspang u. d. Potentiana v. Ober-
burg, † nach 24. VIII. 1567. Kinder: a) aus 1. Ehe:
1) Adam auf Frauenberg u. Winteriz, erhielt 1563 mit
Ges.-Art. 77 das ungar. Indigenat, † auf der Insel
Schinta in Ungarn, ✕ I) mit Margareta, T. d. Adam
des Aelt. v. Sternberg auf Blatná, Blowitz, Grünberg,
Hanfstengel, Klenau, Konopischt, Nepomuk, Alt-Pilse-
netz u. Planitz u. d. Margareta Malowetz v. Malowitz
a. d. H. Patzau; II) mit Elisabeth, T. d. Alexius
Thurzó v. Bethlenfalva u. d. Magdalena Székely v.
Kövend a. d. H. Ratkowdol, † 29. XI. 1573 (wae ✕ in
1. Ehe mit Jaroslaus v. Pernstein auf Helfenstein u.
wieder ✕ in 3. Ehe 1567 mit Julius Gfen zu Salm u.
Neuburg am Inn auf Schwadorf, Ladendorf, Gross-Paw-
lowitz u. Göding, † 2. VII. 1595, ⚰ Stiftskirche bei
St. Dorothea Wien). — 2) Maria Margareta, † 3. I.
1573, ✕ nach 1540 mit Erasmus v. Windisch-Graetz
RFrhrn zu Waldstein u. im Thal, † 1. II. 1573, beide
⚰ bei den Dominikanern Graz. — b) aus 2. Ehe: 3)
David, w. f. — 4) Johann, 1559, † um 1561. — 5)
Anna Maria, ✕ I) 1569 mit Julius Schlik RGfen
zu Bassano auf Rabenstein, † 1575; II) mit Heinrich
Schlik RGfen zu Bassane anf Plan, Welechow, Hauen-
stein u. Himmelstein, † 24. II. 1585. — c) aus 3.
Ehe: 6) Potentiana.

XII. David Ungnad RFrhr zu Sonnegg auf Bleiburg, Rektor der Universität Wittenberg, kais. Geb. Rat
u. Hofkriegsratspräs. a. D. u. Koår bei den Verhand-
lungen zu Kaschau, Landstand in Oe. ob der Enns 1566,
1586 in den n.-ö. alten Hstd aufgen., erhielt 1593
mit Ges.-Art. 23 das ungar. Indigenat, † Kaschau 22.
XII. 1600, ⚰ Horn, ✕ Vöcklamarkt 18. I. 1579 mit
Eva, T. d. Lukas Lang v. Wellenburg auf Kitzbühel u.
d. Maria Elisabeth RFreiin v. Thannhausen a. d. H.
Gradenegg. Kinder: (1) Christof, † unverm. — (2)

Adam, † unverm. — (3) Andreas, w. f. — (4) Georg, †
unverm. — (5) Elisabeth Magdalena, † Ortenburg in
Bayern 1631, ✕ auf Efferding 1. II. 1597 mit Erasmus
dem Aelt. RGfen v. Starhemberg auf Schaumberg,
Riedegg, Wildberg u. Lobenstein, † auf Gstöttenau 14.
VII. 1648, ⚭ Helmonsödt. — (6) Eufemia, † Neu-
haus in Böhmen 1632 unverm. — (7) Katharina, † unverm.

XIII. Andreas Ungnad RFrhr zu Sonnegg auf Ennsegg u. Waldenstein, † Emden 1623, ✕ Linz 16. IX.
1601 mit Maria Margareta Barbara, Erbt. d. Friedrich v. Prag Frhrn zu Windhag auf Engelstein u. d.
Elisabeth RFreiin v. Rogendorf auf Mollenburg a. d. H.
Sitzendorf, † Linz 13. IX. 1669. Kinder: 1. David,
w. f. — 2. Helena, † unverm. — 3. Elisabeth Margareta, ✕ I) 1632 mit Anton Günther RGfen v.
Oldenburg u. Delmenhorst, gesch. 1635, † 19. VI.
1667; II) mit Johann v. Marenholtz. — 4. Eva Elisabeth, ✕ Emden mit Johann Reinhad Ehren-
reuter zu Hofreith auf Hauskirchen. — 5. Katharina,
† unverm.

XIV. David Ungnad, s. d. Pressburg 3. XI. 1646
unter Verleihung des Palatinates nach dem Rechte der
Erstgeburt RGf u. s. d. Pressburg 7. III. 1647 auch
erbländ. Gf v. Weissenwolff Frhr zu Sonnegg u.
Ennsegg auf Grieskirchen, Kematen, Meggenhofen, Rhainleuthen, Roith u. Spielberg im Machlande u. Rechberg
in N.-O., seit 14. I 1648 Obersterblandhofmeister in Oe.
ob d. E., in das schwäb. RGfenkollegium aufgen. 1652,
Rr d. O. v. gold. Vl., kais. WGR u. Km., ∗ 1604, †
Linz 6. III. 1672, ✕ mit Maria Elisabeth, Erbt. d.
Helmhard Christof Jörger des Jüng. Frhrn zu Tolet,
Köppach u. Kreusbach auf Steyregg, Arnburg, Erlach,
Lustenfelden, Pergau u. Hernals u. d. Maria Magda-
lena v. Polheim a. d. H. Parz, † 24. IV. 1674. Kinder:
1) Leopold Wilhelm, † jung. — 2) Johann David, †
jung. — 3) Ferdinand Wenzel, † jung. — 4) Maria
Margareta, † 1661, ✕ Wien 22. IX. 1652 mit Franz
Ernst Schlik RGfen zu Bassano u. Weisskirchen,
Fkherrn auf Kopidlno, Altenburg, Plan, Hauenstein,
Gottschau u. Kunstadt, † Regensburg 16. VIII. 1675. —

5) Helmhard, w. f. — 6) Katharina Elisabeth, * Wien 10. VIII. 1637.

XV. Helmhard Christof Ungnad RGf v. Weissenwolff Frhr zu Sonnegg u. Ennsegg auf Steyregg, Spielberg, Roith, Rhainleuthen, Parz, Lustenfelden, Luftenberg, Köppach, Kematen, Grieskirchen, Erlach, Gröbming, Rechberg u. Weickartsberg, Obersterblandhofmeister in Oe. ob d. E., Erbschenk des Hochstiftes Passau, kais. WGR u. Km., Rr d. O. v. gold. Vl., erhielt als Pfandinhuber von Carlstein s. d. Wien 24. XI. 1674 das böhm. Inkolat, * 1635, † Linz 19. II. 1702; ✕ I) Wien 23. I. 1656 mit Maria Susanna Frobenia Eufemia Posthuma, T. d. Michael Adolf RGfen v. Althann Frhrn auf der Goldburg zu Murstetten u. d. Maria Eva Elisabeth v. Sternberg auf Ebenthal, Eichhorn u. Zistersdorf, * 28. X. 1636, † 7. I. 1661; II) Wien 24. VI. 1665 mit Franziska Benigna Gfin v. Porcia u. Brugnera, T. d. RFsten Johann Ferdinand Gfen v. Ortenburg u. Mitterburg auf Spittel, Senosetsch u. Prem u. d. Beatrix Benigna Kawka v. Ričan auf Wlaschim, † Augsburg 27. VIII. 1690; III) Wien 25. II. 1691 mit Maria Elisabeth, T. d. Johann Andreas des Jüng. RGfen v. Lengheimb auf Pertlstein, Kapfenstein, Schwarzenegg, Reinthal, Messendorf u. Heidenfeld u. d. Maria Anna Helena Maschwander Freiin v. u. zu Schwanau auf Kranichberg, * Graz 24. I. 1666, † Wien 10. III. 1719 (war wieder ✕ in 2. Ehe Wien 15. VII. 1704 mit Otto Ernst Ehrenreich RGfen v. Abensperg u. Traun auf Eglofs, Altmannstein u. Wolkenburg, Majoratsherrn auf Petronell, Maissau, Rapottenstein, Bisamberg, Braunsberg, Wolfpassing, Bockfliess, Gross-Schweinbarth u. Dross, † Wien 8. IX. 1715, ⚰ bei den Dominikanern). Kinder: (1) Maria Elisabeth Secundina Theresia, * das. 17. IV. 1656, † 1689, ✕ I) das. 3. VI. 1675 mit Michael Franz Ferdinand RGfen v. Althann Frhrn auf der Goldburg zu Murstetten, Grulich, Mittelwalde, Schönfeld, Wölfelsdorf, Priessnitz und Selbits, † Prag 2. IV. 1677; II) mit Oktavius Karl RGfen Cavriani Frhrn zu Unterwaltersdorf auf Haus, Pragstein, Kreuzen u. Arbing, † nach 1689. — (2) Leopold Michael Fortunat, * Wien 21. IV. 1657. — (3) Michael Wenzel Franz Josef Januarius Ungnad

RGf v. Weissenwolff Frhr zu Sonnegg u. Ennsegg, *
Wien 14. IX. 1658, † 1679, × das. 17. I. 1678 mit
Ernesta Barbara RGfin v. Montecuccoli, T. d.
RFsten Raimund Hzgs v. Amalfi auf Gleiss, Hain-
dorf, Hohenegg, Osterburg u. Pottendorf u. d. Maria
Margareta Josefa RGfin v. Dietrichstein Freiin zu
Finkenstein, Hollenburg u. Thalberg a. d. H. Nikolsburg,
* Wien 25. V. 1663, † das. 6. V. 1701, ⚰ bei den
Schotten, Stkrd. (war wieder × in 2. Ehe 1680 mit Franz
Christof Khevenhüller v. Aichelberg RGfen zu Fran-
kenburg Frhrn auf Landskron, Wernberg, Hohen-Oster-
witz u. Karlsberg, Majoratsherrn auf Sumeregg, Kammer,
Kogl. Unterach u. Weyregg, † 11. IX. 1684, u. in 3. Ehe
15. I. 1688 mit Wolfgang Andreas RGfen v. Orsini u.
Rosenberg Frhrn auf Lerchenau, Grafenstein, Greifen-
burg, Rottenstein, Keutschach, Welzenegg, Sonnegg,
Höhenbergen, Stein, Rechberg u. Loretto, † Wien 21. X.
1695). Tochter: Maria Theresia Franziska Antonia
Christina auf Wlaschim, * Prag 27. XI. 1678, † im April
1741, × Wien 24. VII. 1694 mit Johann Leopold
Donat RFsten Trautson Gfen zu Falkenstein Frhrn zu
Sprechenstein u. Schroffenstein auf Matrei, Kaya, Laa,
Goldegg, Pielachhaag, Aggsbach, Friesing, Martinitz,
Kralowitz, Hammerstadt, Cechtitz, Křivsoudow, Geblersdorf, Zahrádka, Kalischt, Neuschloss, Böhm.-Rudoletz,
Sárospatak u. Kegécz, † auf St. Pölten 18. X. 1724, ⚰
bei den Barnabiten zu St. Michael Wien. — (4) Katharina Gertraud, † Spangenberg 17. III. 1728, × 1685 mit
Georg Anton Felix Philipp RGfen v. Arco, † Melsungen
8. I. 1709. — (5) Franziska Beatrix, * Wieu 29. X. 1666.
— (6) Margareta, * das. 22. XII. 1667. — (7) Josef
Anton, † im Mai 1692. — (8) Maria Anna, † 1½ Jahre alt
das. 16. VI. 1673. — (9) Maria Josefa Ruberta, * 1673,
† das. 3. V. 1743, × 1. II. 1698 mit Wenzel Adrian
Wilhelm Anton Gfen v. Enkevoirt, Fkherrn auf Gra-
fenegg, Grafenwörth, Schönberg, Gedersdorf, Ober-See-
barn, Bierbaum, Neuaigen, Thürnthal, Walkersdorf, Le-
detsch u. Namiest, † Wien 20. VIII. 1738, ⚰ bei den
Kapuzinern zwischen Krems u. Stein. — (10) Franz
Anton Ungnad RGf v. Weissenwolff Frhr zu Sonnegg
u. Ennsegg auf Steyregg, Erlach, Köppach, Pernau auf
der Haid, Roith, Parz, Spielberg, Lustenfelden, Luften-

berg, Rechberg u. Wlaschim, Obersterblandhofmeister in
Oe. ob d. E., kais. Km. u. RHofrat, * 1679, † Linz zwi-
schen 19. u. 26. II. 1715, ⚰ bei den Jesuiten das., ×
Wien 26. V. 1702 mit Maria Franziska Isabella An-
tonia Sibylla, T. d. Kaspar Friedrich RGfen v. Lam-
berg Frhrn zu Ortenegg u. Ottenstein auf Kunstadt u. d.
Franziska Theresia Freiin Hieserle v. Chodau a. d. H.
Želibořitz, * 8. VII. 1682, † 1748. Tochter: Maria Anna
Josefa, kais. Hofdame u. Stkrd., * 1703, † 16. III.
1730, × Wien 23. IV. 1722 mit Johann Wilhelm Franz
Xaver Anton Balthasar Eduard RFsten Trautson Gfen
zu Falkenstein Frhrn zu Sprechenstein u. Schroffenstein,
Majoratsherrn auf Matrei, Raspenbühel, Poisbrunn, Kaya,
Laa, St. Pölten, Fladnitz, Seyring, Goldegg, Pielach-
haag, Friesing, Aggsbach, St. Pantaleon, Steinbach, Gröb-
ming, Grünburg, Martinitz, Kralowitz, Hammerstadt,
Cechtitz, Křivsoudow, Wlaschim, Geblersdorf, Zahrádka,
Neuschloss, Böhm.-Rudoletz, Sárospatak u. Regécz, †
Wien 31. X. 1775, ⚰ Pfarrkirche St. Michael. —
(11) Ferdinand, w. f. s. u. Aelt. Ast. — (12) Anton, w. f. s. u. Jüng. Ast. — (13) Maria Anna, Stkrd,
* 17. VIII. 1696, † Graz 7. V. 1753, × I) Wien 9. X.
1714 mit Johann Georg Wilhelm RGfen Galler v.
Schwarzeneg Frhrn auf Schwamberg, Waldschach u. Lan-
nach, † Graz 29. X. 1729; II) 2. XI. 1731 mit Ferdinand Leopold RGfen Breunner Edlem Herrn auf Staatz
Frhrn zu Stübing, Fladnitz u. Rabenstein, † 1. IV.
1767.

Aelterer Ast: Erlach.

XVI. Ferdinand Bonaventura Ungnad RGf v.
Weissenwolff Frhr zu Sonnegg u. Ennsegg, Fkherr auf
Erlach, Parz, Grieskirchen, Kematen, Rhainleuthen, Pram,
Wokschitz u. Bartoschow, Obersterblandhofmeister in Oe.
ob d. E., Erbschenk des Hochstifts Passau, k. k. WGR
u. Km., * 29. I. 1693, † Wien 30. XII. 1781, × 26. XI.
1716 mit Maria Theresia Barbara Franziska Josefa
Eustachia, T. d. Thomas Gundacker RGfen v. Starhemberg auf Eschelberg, Lichtenhag, Rottenegg, Oberwallsee, Haus, Freistadt, Ebenfurth, Reichenstein, Senftenberg, Zöbing, Pottendorf, Weigelsdorf, Nagy-Oroszi u.
Hatvan u. d. Beatrix Franziska Maria.

Finding People in the Present

Dead or Alive?

There is a myriad of reasons why you might want to locate someone that you believe is living somewhere in North America. This section will cover techniques for finding people living in the present, both here and in many other countries.

If the person you seek was living in the U.S., then before going through a sequence of searches to find him or her in the present, you should first check to see if that person has died recently. For example, you may be trying to locate an old friend that you went to school with when you were a child.

The Social Security Death Index (SSDI) is maintained in the U.S. Social Security Administration's Death Master File.

The names include anyone who had a Social Security Number (SSN) and whose death was reported to Social Security Administration, and if benefits were payable to the surviving spouse. It contains applications beginning at the end of 1936, although the vast majority of records are for those who died between 1965 and the present. It is updated annually.

Currently, my personal favorite free source of this index is maintained at www.newenglandancestors.org. Updated to 2005, the SSDI contains the names of about 75 million people. The exact address for the SSDI is:

http://www.newenglandancestors.org/database_ search/ssdi.asp

If you find the person you seek, you can also order a copy of their original SSN application form. That application usually shows the full name (and in the case of women, their maiden name), place of birth, date of birth, their address at the time of application, color, the names of parents including the maiden name of the mother, and the signature of the applicant. The signature is very important for comparing to wills, deeds and other important documents the deceased may have signed.

Once you locate data in the SSDI, you can then order a copy of the Application for a Social Security Number (SS-5). To request a copy of a SS-5 form, you must send a letter to the Social Security Administration (pursuant to the *Freedom of Information Act)* with the details of the individual in question. Your letter must include: the name of the individual, the social security number, date and place of death and reason the information is wanted (family history is an acceptable reason). You will need to inquire what the charge is—fees have been rising. Send your letter to:

> Social Security Administration
> Freedom of Information Officer
> 4-H-8 Annex Building
> 6401 Security Blvd.
> Baltimore, MD 21235

One last search you might want to do, however, before searching for a living person, is to check out www. interment.net for cemetery listings, especially if you know the likely state or a tri-state area where he or she might have died.

Once you have carried out the SSDI search, if you do not find a record indicating death and benefits, then it is quite possible that the person you are seeking is actually alive today. In that case, the following section will prove most useful. Finding an old friend from years ago, or finding a long-lost relative, can be a very exciting experience.

U.S. - Searching for a Living Person

A recent and very powerful search used by governments, lawyers, businesses, professional skip tracers and individuals is available at

www.zabasearch.com

Free search results will often include the last several addresses of an individual. In many cases it often reveals the birth year, month or date so you can use a process of elimination to zero in on the person you seek.

Another bonus—search results will often include telephone numbers (don't be surprised to see both listed and unlisted numbers).

Zabasearch claims that this free public information is collected from phone listings, court records, real property records, subscriptions etc. In other words, they claim that their sources are publicly available government records and commercial sources.

For those with an investigative trait, Zabasearch offers a background check for a fee, which may provide a lot of information about an individual.

Once you have the street address in Zabasearch, you can go to www.terraserver.com for a satellite image of the area. To get driving instructions and road maps, go to the popular www.mapquest.com. This is also a very useful website if you are vacationing anywhere in the U.S. and Canada.

New and impressive technology will soon be available from www.pictometry.com. They will be able to provide images of buildings and homes in 3D technology with 45-degree angle photography. A sample is available on the website. It will provide excellent visualization for 911 emergency calls as well as an unlimited number of other uses.

Although zaba means free, this search may not be free in the near future. I would not be surprised to see an annual subscription fee or minimum annual purchase of one background check per year, for example - time will tell. At the time of writing this website search is in beta or testing mode and is free unless you want a background search.

Other websites similar in some ways to Zabasearch are:

> www.criminalsearches.com
> www.peoplesearch.com
> www.peoplescanner.com
> www.intelius.com
> www.ussearch.com

More than a decade ago, white and yellow page listings began appearing on the Internet. Today, it is relatively easy to acquire mailing addresses and telephone numbers along with postal or zip codes.

Telephone Directories Worldwide

Websites that cover white and yellow pages in the U.S. or Canada or both include:

www.whitepages.com
http://www.superpages.com/?SRC=insp
www.411.com
www.switchboard.com

In England and the UK, check out www.192.com which as well as directories, has an amazing set of electoral rolls covering the years 2002 to 2008. These even allow investigators to verify the ages of people in some years. I'm certain that these kinds of searches will be in strong demand in the future in many other countries.

To locate telephone directories in other countries, I will first assume you have read the section on search engines. If so, then the easiest way is to use a search engine and enter white pages Sweden, for example. In some countries, what we call white pages (in North America) are actually known as yellow pages in some other countries, so the alternative technique is to enter into a search engine yellow pages followed by the name of the country. Experiment with naming a large city rather than a country if you have no success.

Contacting people by telephone is not all that expensive compared to years ago, and costs have been coming down thanks to websites like www.magicjack.com and www.jaxtr.com. Remember too that people having the same surname and living in the same area as the person you seek may know the person you're looking for. I've used white page searches effectively many times over the past two decades. Often this search has located the person I was seeking after all other search techniques had failed.

What if you don't know the surname?

Believe it or not, there is a way of searching for someone if you don't have a surname, or if you have forgotten the surname. It is a simple three-step process that is easy once you know how!

(1.) Go to www.intelius.com and select a state, enter the first name and if you know the initial for the middle name enter it also. The more information you can supply, the better. Also, a rare or unusual given name will produce a manageable list of search results.

(2.) Search. The results can then be examined. You will see a list of people with the first names and initials you provided, along with their actual surnames. You may recognize the surname if you have forgotten it, but even if you don't, you have a list of possible names to check out. And how do you check them out? Copy the list or print it out on a sheet of paper, and proceed to the next step.

(3.) Go to www.411.com and enter the full name details you now have, and the state. The search results usually provide you with the full address and telephone number in most instances.

If you find who you are looking for, you can call them to ensure you have the right person and not someone else who just happens to have the same name as the person you seek. Don't ever make assumptions about this. Once you think you have found the right person, you can go back to www.intelius.com and order a background search to see if you have a match (former addresses, etc.).

This search technique works well at the time of writing, but may not be available in the future. The future is uncertain, however, so there may actually be several ways of carrying out this type of search.

Searching for the Living: Worldwide

Another way of finding someone living today is to use quotation marks around the person's name (include their middle name or initial if you have it) in a search engine. Search engine techniques are outlined in a previous chapter. This is a very powerful search, global in its scope, and should never be overlooked. Also, use the advanced features in the search engine to narrow your search even more. If you don't use the advanced features you are not doing the best job of searching.

Your next step would be to check newspapers. The chapter, Finding People in the Past, ends with a careful outline of how to locate newspapers in any country, and more importantly, how to search digital newspapers online. Since many of the newspapers are indexed by every name, up to the present date, you can search for a living person, either today (literally), or during the last decade, for example.

Digital newspapers with digital indexes to every name mentioned therein are a very new type of resource that will have a profound effect on all researchers and biographers in the near future. While many genealogists are using them already, chances are the number of people using this technique will grow rapidly. Many people alive today, including those who might be called hermits or obscure citizens by others, can be located in this manner.

Dead or Alive in Canada

Zabasearch does not currently extend into Canada, but one website that caters to companies as clients to carry out background checks, credit reports and criminal records is www.backcheck.net.

In Canada, nothing similar to the SSDI exists for public access yet, but there are excellent indexes to cemeteries, the most notable of which are the OCFA5 and OCFA6 (Ontario Cemetery Finding Aid) and the BCCFA (British Columbia Cemetery Finding Aid).

Ontario is the most populated province and the OCFA5 and OCFA6 are indexes to people buried in Ontario.

One major disadvantage is that it does not include the date or year of burial. While this is a serious missing piece of data, this search does provide a great benefit to persons who had either uncommon surnames or given names. Also, if you know the county where an ancestor might be buried, this search is very helpful. The city of Toronto is not covered very well in the OCFA search, but Mt. Pleasant Cemetery and its associated cemeteries have very complete computerized records on site.

The OCFA search has the names of more than three million people. To search, go to:

www.islandnet.com/ocfa

The BCCFA is similar, but it does contain dates. It is very valuable for locating burials in British Columbia. This is a free search of the burial records of 344,000 people, and is available from:

www.islandnet.com/bccfa

The Alberta Genealogical Society has been indexing cemeteries throughout the province and will do limited searches for a $2 fee at the time of writing. Check for updates at:

http://abgensoc.ca/nameindex.html

New Brunswick has more than 217,000 cemetery records available. They are located at:

> http://archives.gnb.ca/APPS/NBCemeteries/
> Default.aspx?L=EN&PageLoad=Form

Genealogical Societies

In each province, genealogical societies and their branches have indexed many of the cemeteries in their district or county, often with full extracts and dates. The advantage is that you usually find the person you seek along with other family members mentioned on the gravestone or on a cluster of family stones.

Large Libraries

If you live in Canada, then sizeable regional libraries, provincial libraries, and provincial archives have extensive collections of other useful documents.

As well—and always worthy of note—the Metropolitan Toronto Reference Library (MTRL) is Canada's largest public reference library. It has an excellent collection of records covering many provinces, and in fact, many countries.

Their catalog of holdings as well the holdings of all other Toronto Public Libraries can be accessed at:

http://www.torontopubliclibrary.ca/.

Also in Toronto, the North York Public Library has a very large collection of genealogical books and films covering most of Canada. They can be reached at:

http://www.torontopubliclibrary.ca/uni_can_index.jsp.

And now, let's step into the future together.

The Future Internet

Where is the Internet headed in the future?

I provided an answer to this years ago, in the first edition of this book, and the answer remains so simple that it is almost elusive to the experts.

If you can speak with a child, or if you can think for a moment like a teenager, the answer is plainly evident.

If you ask a child when he would like to hear his favorite song he will say right now. If you needed to know the population of a country for a paper you are writing, you want it now. This idea of the instant world has led us to calling young people The Now Generation.

What we want is now.

If you extrapolate that and look at the World Wide Web and picture it as the source of instant everything, then you will see where the web is going. Some corporations and governments may arrive struggling, kicking and screaming, but they will be inevitably dragged along by the people towards the eventual outcome: Instant information, instant media, the past and the present— all available, now.

Already television cable companies have responded to this public pressure – you and your family may want to watch a certain movie at 6 p.m., stop the movie for supper at 7 p.m., start it up again at 8 p.m. and put it on pause while you get a snack, take a break, or when you want to create your own intermission.

In this case, the media is bending to your timetable and needs, instead of forcing you to bend to an artificial timetable that is not related to, nor cognizant of, your personal needs.

People don't want to build their lives around the media, they want the media to be responsive to their desires at the very moment they want it. And it is already headed in that direction. Convergence will escalate into new territory.

If it is cheap enough or freely included in a monthly service fee, the public will respond. Google learned this early, as well as other websites, large and small. The Internet has proved this time and time again, and created many millionaires simply because they caught sight of what the people wanted, and they met these needs.

All music, all motion pictures, all history, all geography, all education, all art, all music, all art forms, all knowledge, will be wanted on that instant basis. That is the ultimate goal of the future Internet.

If a teacher is world famous because students find him or her to be one of the best, then why shouldn't a million people be able to tune in to that inspiring teacher and repeat the lesson or speed it up, based on their own progress? Why shouldn't they learn at their own speed and still be able to gather in groups and forums and socialize with others?

This is the most probable desired future, and we are moving rapidly in that direction.

In the 1980s, I was told that a patent of a new invention in Europe would take an average of five years before U.S. researchers became aware of it. This was called the technology gap. Now that five-year gap is almost instantaneous.

Several thousand years ago, the prophet Daniel predicted that the day would come when

> …knowledge would cover the earth as the waves cover the sea.

In 1947 and again in a reprinted edition in 1960, Philip Wylie, in his book, *An Essay on Morals,* stated,

> American or Russian, Chinaman, Jap, Hindu, or Briton - we are all on this same planet which has become boat-sized (all) of a sudden.[1]

In 1962, Marshall McLuhan, in his book, *The Gutenberg Galaxy,* wrote about a global electronic village where he envisioned a shared information space—an invisible place where space and time were no longer barriers to acquiring knowledge.[2]

That time is now, and for better rather than worse, the personal computer and the Internet may eventually become the communicative glue that helps to link mankind into a fabric of oneness, creating a new bond of kinship that would include all races, cultures, sciences and religions.

NOTES

[1] Wylie, Philip, An Essay on Morals, Pocket Books, Cardinal Edition, 1960, Chapter 1, page 9. Note: the original Rinehart edition was published in January, 1947.

[2] McLuhan, Marshall. The Gutenber Galaxy: The Making of Typographic Man. New York, N.Y: New American Library, 1969.

The Worldwide Website Directory

The balance of this book contains a directory of several thousand websites, located in more than 250 countries, states and provinces. To create this directory, over 25,000 websites were visited and examined.

If you spend just a few minutes reading the instructions below, and you will be searching like a professional in minutes.

(1) First, select the country, or religious group, or ethnic group you wish to research, and you are on your way. If you have (or can borrow) a scanner with OCR capability, you can scan your chosen list, and then change the scanned image into digital text. That's the key.

(2) Then, copy your digital list of websites into an email. Then, at the very end of each website link, press the enter button on your keyboard, and you should instantly create a hyperlink. Continue down the list changing each website address into a link.

(3) Then, send the email to yourself. When it arrives, you can then click on any link and travel instantly to the selected website. Another way to accomplish the same thing would be to copy the web links you created

in your email, into a Word document instead, for easy reference.

As you know, websites URLs can change, so over time from this publication date there will be some updating required to keep things current in the website directory.

Please note that the directory will be regularly updated through membership in www.grl.com or you can use search engines to add additional websites suitable for your own personal objectives.

Meanwhile, whoever you are looking for, I wish you good hunting!

Worldwide Website Directory

This directory consists of one alphabetical index of addresses for websites, which includes countries, ethnic groups, and religious groups. This compilation is copyrighted and may not be reproduced by any method whatsoever. However, this directory is maintained in up-to-date status for members of www.grl.com where instant links direct you to each site for rapid searching.

Aboriginal Peoples
(see Native Peoples)

Acadian

http://www.acadian-cemeteries.acadian-home.org:80/
    frames.html
www.acadian-cajun.com
www.acadian.org
www.collections.ic.gc.ca/acadian/english/eroots/eroots.htm
www.vivelacajun.com
www.geocities.com/strivingmom/belleile.html
www.perso.wanadoo.fr/le.perto/2acadie1.htm
http://pilot.familysearch.org/recordsearch/start.html#p=0
www.familysearch.org
www.archives.gnb.ca
www.grl.com
www.blupete.com
www.canadiana.org/ECO/mtq?id=a6450175ac&doc=12359

www.genealogie.com

www.islandregister.com

www.umfk.maine.edu/archives/

http://cgi2.cvm.qc.ca/glaporte/1837.pl?cat=ptype&cherche=
BIOGRAPHIE

www.genealogie.umontreal.ca/en/accesLibreBD.htm

www.terriau.org/welcome_english.htm#Home

www.acadian-cajun.com/genac1.htm

members.aol.com/GFSJudi/Acadiansurnam.html

www.gregor.ca/Indexes/acadia-surnamesindex.htm

http://members.tripod.com/~kjunkutie/origins.htm#Acadia

www.lvo.com/MAG/GENEALOGIE.HTML

http://ourworld.compuserve.com/homepages/lwjones/
indefran.htm

www.umoncton.ca/etudeacadiennes/centre/cea.html

www.grl.com

http://philippe.caillebeau.free.fr/recensement.htm

http://perso.wanadoo.fr/froux/

www.ustanne.ednet.ns.ca/cacadien/genealogie.htm

http://epf.planete.qc.ca/base/

www.francogene.com/acadia/index.php

http://cyberquebec.ca/famille-acadienne

www.grandcolombier.com/2003-histoire/acadie/galere.html

www.secondenation.com

www.museeacadien.ca/french/archives/index.htm

www.gov.ns.ca/nsarm/cap/acadian/

www.umoncton.ca/etudeacadiennes/centre/bon-com.htm

www.umoncton.ca/etudeacadiennes/centre/white/sha.html

www.umoncton.ca/etudeacadiennes/centre/memramcook/
mem-lis.htm

www.geocities.com/Heartland/8787/b1868-69.htm

www.pinette.net/genealogy/lk-acad.html

www.umoncton.ca/etudeacadiennes/centre/white/sha.html
http://collections.ic.gc.ca/louisbourg/genealogy/index.html
http://upperstjohn.com/aroostook/deane-kavanagh.htm
http://upperstjohn.com/1820/index.htm
www.geocities.com/Heartland/Acres/2162/
www.umce.ca/biblio/cdem/livres/index.htm
http://users.adelphia.net/~frenchcx/frsurnm1.htm
www.newenglandancestors.org/research/Database/cemeteries/
    default.asp
www.umoncton.ca/etudeacadiennes/centre/cea.html
http://acim.umfk.maine.edu/
www.ustanne.ednet.ns.ca/cacadien/genealogie.htm

Afghanistan

www.world-newspapers.com/
www.uq.net.au/~zzhsoszy/files/gg_index.html
www.rootsweb.com/~afgwgw/
http://pilot.familysearch.org/recordsearch/start.html#p=0
www.familysearch.org
www.museeguimet.fr/gb/homes/home_id20407_u1l2.htm
www.4dw.net/royalark/Afghanistan/durrani7.htm
www.familytreedna.com/surname_join.asp?code=L81323&
    special=True&projecttype=G
www.afghan-network.net/Rulers
www.afghan-network.net/biographies/

Africa
(see also individual countries)

http://garamond.stanford.edu/depts/ssrg/africa/libaf.html
www.africa-research.org/mainframe.html

http://pilot.familysearch.org/recordsearch/start.html#p=0
www.familysearch.org
www.bl.uk/collections/african.html
www.worldvitalrecords.com

African-American

www.afrigeneas.com
www.ibiblio.org/laslave/fields.php
www.aamu.edu/archivemuseumcenter/aboutus/index.html
www.famu.edu/acad/archives
www.af.public.lib.ga.us/aarl/index.html
http://www.afriquest.com/
www.chipublib.org/002branches/woodson/wnharsh.html
www.marquette.edu/library/collections/archives/native_
   writes.html
http://amistadresearchcenter.org/manu-list.cfm
http://pilot.familysearch.org/recordsearch/start.html#p=0
www.familysearch.org
www.pratt.lib.md.us/slrc/afam
www.fhwgs.org
www.blackarchives.org/ba/scope.htm
www.nypl.org/research/sc/sc.html
www.wssu.edu/library/archives/speech.asp
http://library.cincymuseum.org/aag/guide.html
http://astro.ocis.temple.edu/~masante/blockson.html
www.cofc.edu/avery
www.fisk.edu/index.asp?cat=7&pid=257
www.hamptonu.edu/museum/archives.htm
http://memory.loc.gov/ammem
http://209.10.16.21/TEMPLATE/FrontEnd/index.cfm
www.npl.lib.va.us/sgm/oldlobby/afram.html
http://www2.lib.udel.edu/subj/blks/internet/afamarc.htm

Albania

www.world-newspapers.com
www.uq.net.au/~zzhsoszy/files/gg_index.html
www.libdex.com/country.html
www.rootsweb.com/~albwgw
http://pilot.familysearch.org/recordsearch/start.html#p=0
www.familysearch.org
www.fletetebardha.com

Algeria

www.world-newspapers.com
www.libdex.com/country.html
www.pieds-noirs.org
www.geneagm.org/ABCDfrm.htm
www.geneagm.org/
www.archives-dgan.gov.dz
www.editions-gandini.com
http://site.acgc.free.fr
www.geneagm.org
www.geneagm.org/LIENSAGMfrm.htm
www.genealoj.org/ENtexte/page132.html
www.arabinfoseek.com/algeria.htm
www.genealogie-gamt.org/index2.asp
www.africa-research.org/mainframe.html

American Samoa

www.oneworld.net/article/country/16
www.linkpendium.com/genealogy/USA/AS
www.accessgenealogy.com/samoa
www.rootsweb.com/~samoawgw

http://pilot.familysearch.org/recordsearch/start.html#p=0
www.familysearch.org
www.ashpo.org

Andorra

www.world-newspapers.com
www.libdex.com/country.html
http://members.aol.com/mrosado007/andorra.htm
www.italysoft.com/utility/andorra.html
http://pilot.familysearch.org/recordsearch/start.html#p=0
www.familysearch.org
www.arxius.ad

Anglican Church
(Canada, Australia New Zealand & Polynesia)

www.rootsweb.com/~canns/anglican.html
http://aabc.bc.ca/aabc/anglican.html
http://aabc.bc.ca/aabc/angdkoo.html
http://library.mcmaster.ca/archives/anglican/diocese/g.html
http://ngb.chebucto.org/Research/st_thomas.shtml
www.archivists.org.au/directory/data/231.htm
www.anglican.org.nz/Resources/Archives1.htm
www.episcopalarchives.org/genealogy.html
www.archives.gov.on.ca/english/interloan/v-bkofmarriages.htm
www.manl.nf.ca/hrdarchives.htm
www.trinity.utoronto.ca/Library/special.htm

Angola

www.world-newspapers.com
www.libdex.com/country.html

www.africa-research.org/mainframe.html
http://pilot.familysearch.org/recordsearch/start.html#p=0
www.familysearch.org

Anguilla

http://pilot.familysearch.org/recordsearch/start.html#p=0
www.familysearch.org
www.candoo.com/genresources

Antigua and Barbuda

www.world-newspapers.com
www.candoo.com/genresources
http://www.rootsweb.ancestry.com/~atgwgw/
http://pilot.familysearch.org/recordsearch/start.html#p=0
www.familysearch.org

Antilles Françaises
(see also Guadaloupe and Martinique)

www.candoo.com/genresources
http://pilot.familysearch.org/recordsearch/start.html#p=0
www.familysearch.org

Arab World
(see specific country)

Arctic

www.spri.cam.ac.uk/library/archives
http://pilot.familysearch.org/recordsearch/start.html#p=0
www.familysearch.org

Argentina

www.world-newspapers.com
www.libdex.com/country.html
www.mininterior.gov.ar/agn
www.ecomchaco.com.ar/cultura/archivo.htm
www.bapro.com.ar/museo/museo_detgral.htm
http://pilot.familysearch.org/recordsearch/start.html#p=0
www.familysearch.org
http://immigrantships.net/irish_arg/irish_arg1822_29.html
http://www.sisbi.uba.ar/
www.h-net.org/~latam/archives/buenosaires.html

Armenia

www.world-newspapers.com
www.ist.uwaterloo.ca/~marj/genealogy/children/
    Children1927.html
www.libdex.com/country.html
http://pilot.familysearch.org/recordsearch/start.html#p=0
www.familysearch.org
www.matenadaran.am

Aruba

www.world-newspapers.com
http://pilot.familysearch.org/recordsearch/start.html#p=0
www.familysearch.org

Asia
(see specific country)

www.affho.org
http://www.rootsweb.ancestry.com/~asiagw/
www.nla.gov.au/lap
www.bl.uk/collections/asiapacificafrica.html
www.bl.uk/collections/orientalcollections.html
www.s-asian.cam.ac.uk/libhome.html
www.worldvitalrecords.com

Australia

http://www.naa.gov.au/collection/explore/migration/index.aspx.
www.world-newspapers.com
www.libdex.com/country.html
www.awm.gov.au/research/index.htm
www.doors-to-the-past.com.au/strays.html
www.ausbdm.org
www.bdm.nsw.gov.au
http://freepages.genealogy.rootsweb.ancestry.com/~maddenps/
    TIPPEM1.htm
http://pilot.familysearch.org/recordsearch/start.html#p=0
www.familysearch.org
http://members.iinet.net.au/~perthdps/convicts/index.html
http://members.iinet.net.au/~perthdps/military/index.html
www.affho.org
http://home.pacific.net.au/~dparker/barc.htm
www.archives.tas.gov.au
www.archives.anu.edu.au/nbac/html/index.php
www.awm.gov.au/research/research.htm
www.blacktown.nsw.gov.au/blacktown/index.cfm?1CB664A2-
    BCD9-D616-B203-869ABEFB2006
http://www.brisbane.qld.gov.au/BCC:BASE:1957848534:
    pc=PC_1244

www.castlemainehistoricalsociety.com/page3.html?id=196

www.geelongcity.vic.gov.au/Services_In_Geelong/Archives

http://home.vicnet.net.au/~hhs/archives.htm

www.library.jcu.edu.au/Specials

http://voyager.ocs.mq.edu.au/cgi-bin/Pwebrecon.cgi?DB=
local&PAGE=First

http://www.naa.gov.au/services/family-historians/index.aspx

www.nla.gov.au/collect/rarecoll.html

www.nt.gov.au/dcis/nta

http://www.parracity.nsw.gov.au/culture__and__leisure/
heritage_centre/local_studies__and__family_history_
library

www.penrithcity.nsw.gov.au/index.asp?id=556

www.prov.vic.gov.au/default.asp

www.archives.qld.gov.au

www.rahs.org.au/rahs%20library.html#Special%20collections

http://www.sl.nsw.gov.au/about/collections/

www.slq.qld.gov.au/about/coll/jol

www.slsa.sa.gov.au/site/page.cfm?area_id=15&nav_id=1659

http://www.statelibrary.tas.gov.au/whatdo/services/famhistory

www.slv.vic.gov.au/collections/australiana/index.html

www.liswa.wa.gov.au/battye.html

www.records.nsw.gov.au

http://www.sro.wa.gov.au/index.asp

www.archives.sa.gov.au

www.lib.unimelb.edu.au/collections/archives

www.lib.unimelb.edu.au/collections/special

www.une.edu.au/archives/

www.library.uq.edu.au/fryer/index.phtml#special

www.sag.org.au/

www.archivenet.gov.au/archives.html

www.gabr.net.au/gabr_home.html

www.atua.org.au/atua.htm
www.archivists.org.au/directory/asa_dir.htm
http://immigrantships.net/ww2_au.html
http://www.ancestry.com.au/
www.nla.gov.au/raam
www.bl.uk/collections/oesoz.html
http://censuslinks.com/search.php?what=australia
www.genealogybranches.com/international.html
www.maxpages.com/poland/Census_Research
http://www.ffhs.org.uk/members2/overseas/australia.php

Austria

http://www.eegsociety.org/Home.aspx
https://www.wien.gv.at/grabauskunft/internet/suche.aspx
http://www.digento.de/titel/102564.html
www.world-newspapers.com
www.libdex.com/country.html
http://www.rootsweb.ancestry.com/~autwgw/
www.patscheider.at/start.htm?ahnenforschung.htm
http://sites.huji.ac.il/archives/wienna%20list.htm
http://pilot.familysearch.org/recordsearch/start.html#p=0
www.familysearch.org
www.stadt-salzburg.at/internet/stadtverwaltung/
    kulturschulverwaltun/t2_13715/t2_89893/p2_89913.htm
www.oesta.gv.at/ewelcom.htm
www.doew.at/english/content.html
www.onb.ac.at/sammlungen/hschrift/index.htm
www.onb.ac.at/sammlungen/litarchiv/index.htm
www.kabarettarchiv.at
www.salzburg.gv.at/en/themen/se/salzburg/archive.htm
http://stevemorse.org/

www.graz.at
www.eisenstrasse.info/schatzsuche/schatzsucher/archiv/
    archiv_waidhofen.shtml
http://immigrantships.net/austria_poland_galicia1889.html
www.wels.at/magistrat/magistrat/main_content.asp?ds_id=24
http://ub.uni-graz.at/sosa/index.html
http://www2.uibk.ac.at/ub/hb/ass
www.vorarlberg.gv.at/vorarlberg/bildung_schule/bildung/
    landesarchiv/start.htm#
www.oesta.gv.at/deudiv/arch_oe.htm
http://home.bawue.de/~hanacek/info/aarchive.htm
www.genealogienetz.de/reg/AUT/austria.html
http://hlt.at/
www.genealogie.co.at

Austro-Hungarian Empire

http://homepages.rootsweb.ancestry.com/~andert/pomogy.htm
http://pilot.familysearch.org/recordsearch/start.html#p=0
www.familysearch.org
http://stevemorse.org/

Azerbaijan

www.world-newspapers.com
http://pilot.familysearch.org/recordsearch/start.html#p=0
www.familysearch.org
www.libdex.com/country.html

Bahai (Baha'i)

http://library.bahai.org/sc/index.html

http://www.planetbahai.org/cgi-bin/main.pl
www.bahai-faith.org
www.bahai.org.za
www.bahai.co.zw

Bahamas

www.world-newspapers.com
www.libdex.com/country.html
www.candoo.com/genresources
www.bahamasnationalarchives.bs
http://pilot.familysearch.org/recordsearch/start.html#p=0
www.familysearch.org
http://www.rootsweb.ancestry.com/~bhswgw/

Bahrain

www.world-newspapers.com
www.uq.net.au/~zzhsoszy/files/gg_index.html
http://pilot.familysearch.org/recordsearch/start.html#p=0
www.familysearch.org
www.libdex.com/country.html
www.uob.bh/

Bangladesh

www.world-newspapers.com
www.libdex.com/country.html
http://www.rootsweb.ancestry.com/~bgdwgw/
http://pilot.familysearch.org/recordsearch/start.html#p=0
www.familysearch.org
http://genealogy.about.com/cs/india

Baptists

www.gendocs.demon.co.uk/bapt.html
www.rootsweb.com/~usgenweb/me/baptist/freewill/files.html
www.sbhla.org
http://davisweb.samford.edu/about/special.html
www.abc-usa.org/abhs
www.macdiv.ca/students/baptistarchives.php
http://library.acadiau.ca/archives/genresearch.html
www.kybaptist.org/kbc/welcome.nsf/pages/ExecutiveArchives
http://library.cn.edu/baptarch.html
http://home.pacific.net.au/~dparker/barc.htm
www.abc-usa.org/abhs
http://homepages.rootsweb.com/~baptist/collections.html
http://rylibweb.man.ac.uk/data2/spcoll/nbc
http://www.carthage.lib.il.us/community/churches/primbap/
    pbl.html
http://library.furman.edu/staff/contact.htm
www.bgct.org/bgctroot/office.cfm?sectionid=7&officeid=43
www.americanswedishinst.org/archives.htm
www.mc.edu/campus/library/mbhc.htm
www.wfu.edu/Library/special/index.html
http://library.acadiau.ca/archives/genresearch.html
www.abc-usa.org/abhs
http://carolus.furman.edu/depts/speccoll/speccoll.htm
www.baptistheritage.org/modules.php?name=Research
www.hkbu.edu.hk/library/sca/index.html
www.poleungkuk.org.hk/museum/store_e.htm
http://lib.hku.hk/hkspc/index.html
www.c3.hu/%7Emev/tartalom/98_1_2/szebeni.htm
www.sbhla.org/links.htm
www.baptisten.org/start/index.php

Barbados

www.world-newspapers.com
www.barbmuse.org.bb
www.genealogy-quest.com/collections/jamcens.html
www.candoo.com/genresources
http://barbados.org/museum2.htm
http://pilot.familysearch.org/recordsearch/start.html#p=0
www.familysearch.org
www.rootsweb.com/~brbwgw

Belarus

www.eegsociety.org/Index.html
www.world-newspapers.com
www.libdex.com/country.html
http://pilot.familysearch.org/recordsearch/start.html#p=0
www.familysearch.org
www.rootsweb.com/~blrwgw
www.archives.gov.by/eindex.htm
www.mtu-net.ru/rrr/ukraine.htm

Belgium

www.world-newspapers.com
www.libdex.com/country.html
http://geneaknowhow.net/digi/resources.html
http://pilot.familysearch.org/recordsearch/start.html#p=0
www.familysearch.org
http://belgium.rootsweb.com/index.html
http://freepages.genealogy.rootsweb.com/~fkruse/oldsports/
    index.html

http://membres.lycos.fr/numa/assgensurnet.html
http://membres.lycos.fr/hbarnich/genefam.htm
http://www.dijkgraaf.org/benelux.htm
www.infobel.com/world
www.rootsweb.com/~belghist/Flanders/index.htm
http://arch.arch.be
http://www.kbr.be/collections/reserve/reserve_consult_fr.html
www.aequatoria.be/archives_project/English/EGindex.html
www.nato.int/archives/index.htm
http://stadsarchief.antwerpen.be/default.asp
www.brugge.be/archief/index.htm
www.lokeren.be/cultuur/archief.htm
www.sint-niklaas.be/modules/phpwiki/index.php?pagename=
    Stadsarchief
www.sint-pieters-leeuw.be/administratie/stafd_docu_archief.htm
www.leuven.be/showpage.asp?iPageID=957
www.veurne.be/Stadsarchief/2203/default.aspx?id=3193
http://surf.to/BEL-archives
www.censuslinks.com/index
http://geneaknowhow.net/digi/resources.html

Belize

www.world-newspapers.com
www.candoo.com/genresources
http://pilot.familysearch.org/recordsearch/start.html#p=0
www.familysearch.org

Benin

www.world-newspapers.com
www.libdex.com/country.html

www.africa-research.org/mainframe.html
http://pilot.familysearch.org/recordsearch/start.html#p=0
www.familysearch.org

Bermuda

www.libdex.com/country.html
www.candoo.com/genresources
http://pilot.familysearch.org/recordsearch/start.html#p=0
www.familysearch.org
www.rootsweb.com/~bmuwgw/bermuda.htm

Bessarabia
(see also Moldova)

www.eegsociety.org/Index.html
http://pilot.familysearch.org/recordsearch/start.html#p=0
www.familysearch.org

Bhutan

www.world-newspapers.com
www.rootsweb.com/~btnwgw
http://pilot.familysearch.org/recordsearch/start.html#p=0
www.familysearch.org

Blacks
(see African-American)

Bohemia

www.eegsociety.org/Index.html

http://pilot.familysearch.org/recordsearch/start.html#p=0
www.familysearch.org
www.cgsi.org
http://freepages.genealogy.rootsweb.com/~elainetmaddox

Bolivia

www.world-newspapers.com
www.libdex.com/country.html
www.h-net.org/~latam/archives/project3.html
http://pilot.familysearch.org/recordsearch/start.html#p=0
www.familysearch.org

Bosnia and Herzegovina

www.world-newspapers.com
www.arhivrs.org
www.arhivsa.ba
http://pilot.familysearch.org/recordsearch/start.html#p=0
www.familysearch.org

Botswana

www.world-newspapers.com
www.uq.net.au/~zzhsoszy/files/gg_index.html
www.libdex.com/country.html
www.gov.bw/government/ministry_of_labour_and_home_
    affairs.html#national_archives_and_records
www.africa-research.org/mainframe.html
http://pilot.familysearch.org/recordsearch/start.html#p=0
www.familysearch.org

Brazil

www.world-newspapers.com
www.libdex.com/country.html
www.arquivoestado.sp.gov.br
www.rio.rj.gov.br/arquivo
www.arquivonacional.gov.br
www.secult.ce.gov.br/APEC/Apec.asp
www.ape.es.gov.br
www.arqpep.pa.gov.br
www.cpdoc.fgv.br/accessus/htm/ap_oqsap.htm
www.museuhistoriconacional.com.br/ingles/mh-m-2.htm
www.ssac.unicamp.br
www.cedem.unesp.br
www.h-net.org/~latam/archives/brazil.html
www.geocities.com/arquivosmunicipais
http://pilot.familysearch.org/recordsearch/start.html#p=0
www.familysearch.org

Brethren

www.cob-net.org/fobg
www.bridgewater.edu/departments/library/specialcoll/
    #brethren
www.cob-net.org/genhis.htm

British Commonwealth

www.cwgc.org/cwgcinternet/search.aspx
http://pilot.familysearch.org/recordsearch/start.html#p=0
www.familysearch.org
http://www.pricegen.com/english_genealogy.html

British Virgin Islands

www.candoo.com/genresources
http://pilot.familysearch.org/recordsearch/start.html#p=0
www.familysearch.org

Brunei

www.world-newspapers.com
www.uq.net.au/~zzhsoszy/files/gg_index.html
www.libdex.com/country.html
www.brunei.gov.bn
http://pilot.familysearch.org/recordsearch/start.html#p=0
www.familysearch.org

Buddhism

www.shambhalashop.com/archives
http://ccbs.ntu.edu.tw/FULLTEXT/JR-PHIL/ew92864.htm
www.ucpress.edu/books/pages/9995.html
www.cambodianbuddhist.org
www.hsuyun.org/Dharma/zbohy/Home/home-index.html

Bukovina

www.eegsociety.org/Index.html
http://pilot.familysearch.org/recordsearch/start.html#p=0
www.familysearch.org

Bulgaria

www.world-newspapers.com

www.libdex.com/country.html
http://pilot.familysearch.org/recordsearch/start.html#p=0
www.familysearch.org

Burkina Faso

www.world-newspapers.com
www.libdex.com/country.html
http://pilot.familysearch.org/recordsearch/start.html#p=0
www.familysearch.org
www.africa-research.org/mainframe.html

Burma
(Myanmar)

www.uq.net.au/~zzhsoszy/files/gg_index.html
www.rootsweb.com/~mmrwgw/
http://genealogy.about.com/gi/dynamic/offsite.htm?site=
    http%3A%2F%2F
http://pilot.familysearch.org/recordsearch/start.html#p=0
www.familysearch.org
www.ozemail.com.au%2F%7Eclday%2F

Burundi

www.world-newspapers.com
www.uq.net.au/~zzhsoszy/files/gg_index.html
www.libdex.com/country.html
www.africa-research.org/mainframe.html
http://pilot.familysearch.org/recordsearch/start.html#p=0
www.familysearch.org

Cajun

www.bayougenealogy.com
www.acadian-cajun.com
www.geocities.com/~colony
http://ourworld.compuserve.com/homepages/lwjones/
	indefran.htm
www.ghcaraibe.org
www.notarialarchives.org/
http://pilot.familysearch.org/recordsearch/start.html#p=0
www.familysearch.org

Cambodia

www.camnet.com.kh/archives.cambodia
www.world-newspapers.com
www.uq.net.au/~zzhsoszy/files/gg_index.html
www.rootsweb.com/~khmwgw/
www.cambodianbuddhist.org
http://pilot.familysearch.org/recordsearch/start.html#p=0
www.familysearch.org

Cameroon

www.world-newspapers.com
www.libdex.com/country.html
www.africa-research.org/mainframe.html
http://pilot.familysearch.org/recordsearch/start.html#p=0
www.familysearch.org

Canada

(First, this list shows websites that are Canada-wide. Following this list, see also each province listed separately)

www.genealogy.gc.ca

http://www.collectionscanada.gc.ca/genealogy/022-911-e.html

www.cwgc.org/cwgcinternet/search.aspx

www.archivescanada.ca/car/menu.html

http://www.collectionscanada.gc.ca/databases/war-dead/001056-100.01-e.php

http://www.canadiana.org/eco.php?doc=microlib&id=a6f754 0366b91159&page=Initial

http://freepages.genealogy.rootsweb.ancestry.com/~gaelynn/prison.htm

http://pilot.familysearch.org/recordsearch/start.html#p=0

www.familysearch.org

www.ancestry.ca

http://www.united-church.ca/local/archives

www.grl.com

www.world-newspapers.com

http://www.collectionscanada.gc.ca/index-e.html

www.ist.uwaterloo.ca/~marj/genealogy/children/children.html

www.libdex.com/country.html

http://home.att.net/~Local_Catholic/#Select_Location

www.canadiana.org/eco/english/index.html

http://geonames.nrcan.gc.ca/index_e.php

www.mcgill.ca/dcp/

www.ingeneas.com/free/index.html

http://membres.lycos.fr/numa/assgensurnet.html

www2.ville.montreal.qc.ca/biblio/

www.newenglandancestors.org/research/Database/cemeteries/default.asp

www.infobel.com/world

www3.sympatico.ca/bkinnon/obit_links.htm#ab

http://unitedchurcharchives.vicu.utoronto.ca/

www.archivescanada.ca/english/index.html

www.geocities.com/Heartland/Acres/2162/

www.generations.on.ca/genealogy.htm

www.uidaho.edu/special-collections/Other.Repositories.html

www.collectionscanada.ca/collection/index-e.html

http://home.interlog.com/~ucrdc/archives.html

www.library.utoronto.ca/east/

http://www8.cpr.ca/cms/English/General+Public/Heritage/
    Archives.htm

www.hunterinformation.com/corporat.htm

www.astro.uni-bonn.de/~pbrosche/hist_astr/ha_arch.html

www.astro.uni-bonn.de/~pbrosche/hist_sci/hs_arch.html

http://mla-hhss.org/histloca.htm

http://www.collectionscanada.gc.ca/canadiandirectories/

www.sharpweb.org/

http://scriptorium.lib.duke.edu/women/article.html

www.hunterinformation.com/corporat.htm

www.piasa.org/polisharchivesinamerica.html

http://canadianlibgenie.blogspot.com

http://ccgwiki.vpl.ca/index.php/ccg_wiki/Chinese_
    Immigration_List

www.censuslinks.com/index

www.genealogybranches.com/international.html

Canada (by Provinces):

Alberta

http://www.collectionscanada.gc.ca/index-e.html

www.afhs.ab.ca/data/announcements/index.html
http://users.rootsweb.com/~canab/index.html
www.odessa3.org/collections/cemeteries/canada/
http://pilot.familysearch.org/recordsearch/start.html#p=0
www.familysearch.org
www.ancestry.ca
www.grl.com
www.odessa3.org/collections/obits/
www.archivescanada.ca/car/car_e.asp?l=e&a=p&v=1
http://abgensoc.ca
http://calgarypubliclibrary.com/library/local_history.htm
www.glenbow.org/archives.htm
http://collections.ic.gc.ca/riviere-la-paix/societe_
     genealogique/
www.southpeacearchives.org/

British Columbia

www.collectionscanada.ca/archivianet/020111_e.html
www.grl.com
www.bcarchives.gov.bc.ca/textual/general/genealog.htm
www.bcarchives.gov.bc.ca/textual/governmt/vstats/v_events.htm
www.islandnet.com/bccfa/
http://pilot.familysearch.org/recordsearch/start.html#p=0
www.familysearch.org
www.ancestry.ca
www.rootsweb.com/~canbc/
www.archivescanada.ca/car/car_e.asp?l=e&a=p&v=2
www.bcgs.ca/
www.city.vancouver.bc.ca/ctyclerk/archives/
www.richmond.ca/home.htm
www.crowsnest.bc.ca/camal/crharl.html

www.inlofna.org/IABC/Welcome.html
www.sfu.ca/archives/
http://aabc.bc.ca/aabc/archweb.html
http://aabc.bc.ca/aabc/bcguide.html

Labrador
(see Newfoundland & Labrador)

Manitoba

www.collectionscanada.ca/archivianet/020111_e.html
www.gov.mb.ca/chc/archives/hbca/index.html
www.gov.mb.ca/chc/archives/index.html
http://www.mbgenealogy.com
http://pilot.familysearch.org/recordsearch/start.html#p=0
www.familysearch.org
www.ancestry.ca
www.grl.com
http://www.shsb.mb.ca/
www.rootsweb.com/~canmb/index.htm
www.geocities.com/uggncr/
www.archivescanada.ca/car/car_e.asp?l=e&a=p&v=3
http://winnipeg.ca/clerks/docs/archives/archives.stm
www.shsb.mb.ca/englishindex.htm
http://web2.gov.mb.ca/cca/vital/Query.php

New Brunswick

www.newirelandnb.ca/nb_irish_family_names.html
www.archives.gnb.ca/Archives
http://www.acadian-cemeteries.acadian-home.org:80/frames.
   html

http://pilot.familysearch.org/recordsearch/start.html#p=0
www.familysearch.org
www.ancestry.ca
www.grl.com
www.lib.unb.ca/gddm/data/panb/panbweb.html
http://upperstjohn.com/1820/index.htm
www.rootsweb.com/~cannb/
www.umce.ca/biblio/cdem/livres/index.htm
www.rootsweb.com/~nbgfgc/cemetaryindx.html
www.newenglandancestors.org/research/Database/cemeteries/
    default.asp
www.archivescanada.ca/car/car_e.asp?l=e&a=p&v=12
http://archives.gnb.ca/Archives/Default.aspx?L=EN
www.umoncton.ca/etudeacadiennes/centre/archivescum/
    arcum2.html
www.umoncton.ca/etudeacadiennes/centre/arcpri.html
www.lib.unb.ca/archives/

Newfoundland & Labrador

www.grl.com
http://ngb.chebucto.org/index.html
www.rootsweb.com/~cannf/index.html
www.manl.nf.ca/hrdarchives.htm
www.united-church.ca/archives/nfl/home.shtm
www.archivescanada.ca/car/car_e.asp?l=e&a=p&v=4
http://pilot.familysearch.org/recordsearch/start.html#p=0
http://www.newfoundlandgenealogy.com/
www.familysearch.org
www.ancestry.ca
http://ngb.chebucto.org/NGBRIF/
www3.nf.sympatico.ca/nlgs

www.stjohnsarchdiocese.nf.ca/archives.asp
www.stjohns.ca/cityservices/archives/index.jsp
www.library.mun.ca/qeii/cns/archives/cnsarch.php
www.mun.ca/mha/
www.tcr.gov.nl.ca/panl/
www.anla.nf.ca/directory.htm
www.anla.nf.ca/directoryThematic.htm
www.fss.ulaval.ca/etudes-inuit-studies/volu22n1.HTML
www.labradorvirtualmuseum.ca/49

Northwest Territories

www.grl.com
www.rootsweb.com/~cannt/
www.archivescanada.ca/car/car_e.asp?l=e&a=p&v=10
http://pwnhc.learnnet.nt.ca/programs/archive.htm
http://pilot.familysearch.org/recordsearch/start.html#p=0
www.familysearch.org
www.ancestry.ca
http://aabc.bc.ca/aabc/icaul.html

Nova Scotia

https://www.novascotiagenealogy.com/
www.gov.ns.ca/nsarm/cap/genealogy.asp
http://immigrantships.net/halifaxlists/halifaxarr_depart_01.html
http://www.acadian-cemeteries.acadian-home.org:80/frames.
    html
http://www.councilofnsarchives.ca/archway/
www.rootsweb.com/~canns/#DATABASES
http://pilot.familysearch.org/recordsearch/start.html#p=0
http://www.rootsweb.ancestry.com/~nscsheet/baptrecs.html

www.familysearch.org

www.ancestry.ca

http://homepages.rootsweb.ancestry.com/~downhome/nscensus.html

www.grl.com

www.chebucto.ns.ca/~jacktar/privsearch.html

www.rootsweb.com/~canns/nsresources.html

http://www.geocities.com/heartland/farm/7843/cen1770lun1.html

http://www.rootsweb.ancestry.com/~casoccgs/census.html

www.gov.ns.ca/nsarm/databases/bonds

http://homepages.rootsweb.ancestry.com/~capstick/

www.gov.ns.ca/nsarm/databases/land

www.rootsweb.com/~canns/index.html

www.newenglandancestors.org/research/Database/cemeteries/default.asp

www.united-church.ca/archives/maritime/home.shtm

www.chebucto.ns.ca/Recreation/GANS/index.html

http://nsgna.ednet.ns.ca/

www.library.dal.ca/spcol/spcoll.htm

www.go.ednet.ns.ca/~ip96003/gene.html

http://museum.gov.ns.ca/mma/research/research.html#library

www.msvu.ca/library/archives/index.asp

www.gov.ns.ca/nsarm/

www.smu.ca/administration/archives/archives.html

www.ustanne.ednet.ns.ca/cacadien/genealogie.htm

http://yarmouthcountymuseum.ednet.ns.ca/archives.htm

http://www8.cpr.ca/cms/English/General+Public/Heritage/Archives.htm

Nunavut

www.archivescanada.ca/car/car_e.asp?l=e&a=p&v=11
http://genealogy.about.com/od/nunavut/
www.rootsweb.com/~cannt/nunavut.htm
www.nativeamericans.com/Inuit.htm
www.avataq.qc.ca
http://collections.ic.gc.ca/cape_dorset/index1.html
http://college.hmco.com/history/readerscomp/naind/html/
    na_011300_eskimo.htm
http://pilot.familysearch.org/recordsearch/start.html#p=0
www.familysearch.org
www.ancestry.ca
www.grl.com
http://inuit.pail.ca
www.nunavut.com/technology/english/download.html
www.geocities.com/Athens/9479/inuit.html
http://pandora.cii.wwu.edu/vajda/ea210/aleut.htm
www.islandnet.com/~jveinot/cghl/nunavut.html
www.genealogie.gc.ca/07/07070206_e.html
www.fss.ulaval.ca/etudes-inuit-studies/volu22n1.HTML

Ontario

www.ogs.on.ca/ogspi/welcome.htm
http://pilot.familysearch.org/recordsearch/start.html#p=0
www.familysearch.org
www.ancestry.ca
http://www.gravemarkers.ca/
www.grl.com
www.rootsweb.com/~ongenpro/census
www.waterlooogs.ca

www.wellingtonogs.on.ca/2004/
http://www.collectionscanada.gc.ca/the-public/index-e.html
www.ogs.on.ca/ogspi
http://my.tbaytel.net/bmartin/sitemap.htm
www.islandnet.com/ocfa/homepage.html
homepages.rootsweb.com/~maryc/thisisit.htm
www.tpl.toronto.on.ca/localhistory/randr.html
www.geneofun.on.ca/ongenweb
www.100megsfree3.com/granny1/clair1.html
www.uppercanadagenealogy.com/addressesS.html
www.uppercanadagenealogy.com/resources.html
www.archivescanada.ca/car/car_e.asp?l=e&a=p&v=6
www.detroit.lib.mi.us/burton/french_canadian_guide.htm
www.detroit.lib.mi.us/burton/canadian_guide.htm
http://fchsm.habitant.org/
www.archives.gov.on.ca/
www.adarchives.org/
www.brocku.ca/library/spcl/index.htm
www.city.toronto.on.ca/archives/
www.elgin.ca/
http://www.infogo.gov.on.ca/infogo/mainPage.do
www.library.guelph.on.ca/localhistory/
www.collectionscanada.ca/collection/index-e.html
http://library.mcmaster.ca/archives/readyweb.htm
www.tpl.toronto.on.ca/uni_can_index.jsp
www.pcma.ca/archives_agree.htm
http://archives.queensu.ca/
www.region.peel.on.ca/heritage/archives.htm
www.county.simcoe.on.ca/archives.cfm
www.stcatharines.library.on.ca/services/special.htm
www.tbpl.ca/internal.asp?id=87&cid=229
www.trentvalleyarchives.com/tva.htm

www.trinity.utoronto.ca/Library/special.htm
www.uottawa.ca/academic/crccf/resdoc.html
www.library.utoronto.ca/utarms/
www.library.utoronto.ca/east/
www.library.utoronto.ca/fisher/
www.lib.uwo.ca/archives/talman.shtml
http://athena.uwindsor.ca/units/archive/main.nsf
http://library.vicu.utoronto.ca/special/jonesintro.htm
www.wcm.on.ca/archive.php

Prince Edward Island

www.grl.com
www.terriau.org/welcome_english.htm#Home
www.edu.pe.ca/paro/
http://uggpei.isn.net/
www.united-church.ca/archives/maritime/home.shtm
www.archivescanada.ca/car/car_e.asp?l=e&a=p&v=7
www.peigs.ca/
http://pilot.familysearch.org/recordsearch/start.html#p=0
www.familysearch.org
www.ancestry.ca
www.wyattheritage.com/mainsite/macnaught/index.asp
www.edu.pe.ca/paro/research/research.asp
www.upei.ca/library/html/specialcollections.
    html#peicollection

Québec

www.collectionscanada.ca/archivianet/020111_e.html
http://cgi2.cvm.qc.ca/glaporte/1837.pl?cat=ptype&cherche=
    BIOGRAPHIE

www.grl.com

www.genealogie.umontreal.ca/en/accesLibreBD.htm

http://hemcem.sharonmark.com/

http://members.tripod.com/~efortier/

http://cyberquebec.ca/_layout/?uri=http://cyberquebec.ca/
famille-acadienne/

www.sgcf.com/

http://pilot.familysearch.org/recordsearch/start.html#p=0

http://www.voicimafamille.info:80/

www.familysearch.org

www.ancestry.ca

www.genealogie.org/club/sfohg-ottawa/

http://municipalite.yamachiche.qc.ca/toponymie/genealogie/
index.html

www.club-genealogie-longueuil.qc.ca/

www.genealogie.org/club/sglaurentides/

www.rootsweb.com/%7Eqcchatea/cvhs.htm

http://federationgenealogie.qc.ca/

www.rootsweb.com/~canqc/index.htm

www.united-church.ca/archives/mo/home.shtm

www.archivescanada.ca/car/car_e.asp?l=e&a=p&v=8

http://mesaieux.com/an/default.htm

www.sgar.org/

www.ancestry.ca

www.federationgenealogie.qc.ca

www.histoirequebec.qc.ca/

www.bnquebec.ca/portal/dt/accueil.html#

www.detroit.lib.mi.us/burton/french_canadian_guide.htm

www.uottawa.ca/academic/crccf/resdoc.html

http://www2.ville.montreal.qc.ca/chm/engl/centre-doca.shtm

www.etrc.ca/archives.html

www.mcq.org/objets/fonds_archives/index.html

www.rabaska.com/histoire/lacauxsables.htm
www.bib.umontreal.ca/CS/
www.archiv.umontreal.ca/
www.archives.uqam.ca/
www.bibliotheques.uqam.ca/bibliotheques/livres_rares/
    collection.html#col
http://www2.ville.montreal.qc.ca/archives/archives.htm
www.afgs.org/afgsrsrc.html
www.rdaq.qc.ca/
www.rootsweb.com/~canqc/lookups.htm
www.rootsweb.com/~canqc/ressources.htm#societes
http://bibnum2.bnquebec.ca/bna/lovell/index.html
http://simmons.b2b2c.ca/

Saskatchewan

www.saskgenealogy.com
www.collectionscanada.ca/archivianet/020111_e.html
www.rootsweb.com/~cansk/Saskatchewan/
http://pilot.familysearch.org/recordsearch/start.html#p=0
www.familysearch.org
www.ancestry.ca
www.grl.com
www.odessa3.org/collections/cemeteries/canada/
www.odessa3.org/collections/obits/
www.archivescanada.ca/car/car_e.asp?l=e&a=p&v=9
www.saskarchives.com/web/index.html
www.usask.ca/archives/
http://www.city.saskatoon.sk.ca/org/clerks_office/archives/
    index.asp
www.city.saskatoon.sk.ca/org/parks/cemetery/index.asp

Yukon Territories

www.grl.com
http://pilot.familysearch.org/recordsearch/start.html#p=0
www.familysearch.org
www.ancestry.ca
www.rootsweb.com/~canyk/
www.archivescanada.ca/car/car_e.asp?l=e&a=p&v=13
http://aabc.bc.ca/aabc/canwan.html

Cape Verde

www.world-newspapers.com
www.ric.edu/adamslibrary/resources/bibliographies/
   capeverde.html
http://131.128.70.2/search/
   p?SEARCH=cape+verdean+collection
http://pilot.familysearch.org/recordsearch/start.html#p=0
www.familysearch.org
www.africa-research.org/mainframe.html

Caribbean Islands

http://home.att.net/~Local_Catholic/#Select_Location
www.ghcaraibe.org
www.casbah.ac.uk/
http://pilot.familysearch.org/recordsearch/start.html#p=0
www.familysearch.org

Catholic

www.rcab.org/Archives/geneology_resources.html

http://archives.archchicago.org
www.archbalt.org
www.nd.edu/~archives
www.onr.com/user/cat
www.catholic-library.org.uk/registers.html
www.archdiocese-no.org/archives/page4.htm
www.rc.net/philadelphia/pahrc/index.html
www.vatican.va/library_archives/vat_secret_archives/index.htm
www.cgrr.com/contents.htm
www.rootsweb.com/~mikent/mcgee1950/catholicindians.html
http://members.tripod.com/~enlist_1/enlistsearch.htm
www.rootsweb.com/~miwayne/hamtramck.htm
http://home.att.net/~Local_Catholic/#Select_Location
www.rootsweb.com/~canns/catholic.html
www.archivalcenter.org/index.html
www.onr.com/user/cat/
http://libraries.cua.edu/achrcua/index.html
www.jesuit.org/
www.nd.edu/~archives/about.htm
www.xula.edu/library/archives.html
http://bav.vatican.va/en/v_home_bav/v_storia/index.shtml
www.stjohnsarchdiocese.nf.ca/archives.asp
www.pcj.edu/pcjlibrary/Resources.htm#SpecialCollections
http://library.udayton.edu/basics/rarebooks/uscath.php
www.cbu.edu/library/archives/
www.catholiclinks.org/archivescatholiclinks.htm
www.catolicos.org/archives.htm
www.katolsk.no/utenriks/index_en.htm
http://home.att.net/~Local_Catholic/
www.parishesonline.com/scripts/default.asp

Cayman Islands

www.candoo.com/genresources
www.candoo.com/genresources/jamaica.htm
http://pilot.familysearch.org/recordsearch/start.html#p=0
www.familysearch.org

Central African Republic

www.world-newspapers.com
www.libdex.com/country.html
http://lists.rootsweb.com/index/intl/CAF/AFR-CENTRAL-
    AFRICAN-REPUBLIC.html
http://pilot.familysearch.org/recordsearch/start.html#p=0
www.familysearch.org
www.africa-research.org/mainframe.html

Central America
(see specific country)

http://home.att.net/~Local_Catholic/#Select_Location
http://home.att.net/~Local_Catholic/Catholic-CAmerica.htm
http://pilot.familysearch.org/recordsearch/start.html#p=0
www.familysearch.org

Ceylon
(see Sri Lanka)

Chad

www.world-newspapers.com
www.libdex.com/country.html

www.africa-research.org/mainframe.html
http://pilot.familysearch.org/recordsearch/start.html#p=0
www.familysearch.org

Channel Islands

www.genuki.org.uk
www.ancestry.co.uk
http://pilot.familysearch.org/recordsearch/start.html#p=0
www.familysearch.org

Chechnya

www.world-newspapers.com
http://pilot.familysearch.org/recordsearch/start.html#p=0
www.familysearch.org

Czechoslovakia (see Czech Republic)

www.cesarch.cz/adresar.aspx?lang=en
http://pilot.familysearch.org/recordsearch/start.html#p=0
www.familysearch.org

Chile

www.world-newspapers.com
www.libdex.com/country.html
www.bib.udec.cl/bibliotecas/chistoria.htm
www.apellidositalianos.com.ar/archivos_chilenos.htm
http://pilot.familysearch.org/recordsearch/start.html#p=0
www.familysearch.org

China

www.world-newspapers.com/
www.uq.net.au/~zzhsoszy/files/gg_index.html
http://ccgwiki.vpl.ca/index.php/ccg_wiki/Chinese_
    Immigration_List
www.libdex.com/country.html
www.rootsweb.com/~chnwgw
http://pilot.familysearch.org/recordsearch/start.html#p=0
www.familysearch.org
www.library.utoronto.ca/east
www.nlc.gov.cn
www.lib.tsinghua.edu.cn/english/service.html#Ancient%20
    Book%20Service
www.lib.cuhk.edu.hk/information/rarebook/rbroom.htm
www.cityu.edu.hk/lib/collect/prd/index.htm
www.hkbu.edu.hk/library/sca/index.html
www.museeguimet.fr/gb/homes/home_id20407_u1l2.htm
http://orpheus.ucsd.edu/chinesehistory/chinese_archives.htm
www.hsuyun.org/Dharma/zbohy/Home/home-index.html
http://genealogy.about.com/library/authors/ucboey1a.htm

Christian Reformed Church

www.calvin.edu/hh/

Christianity
(see various church groups)

www.home.cio.net/timo/man
www.acns.com/~mm9n/Genealogy/cha1.htm

Church of England

www.episcopalarchives.org/genealogy.html

Churches of God
(see Pentecostal)

Church of Jesus Christ of Latter-Day Saints, The

www.familysearch.org
http://pilot.familysearch.org/recordsearch/start.html#p=0

Church of the Nazarene

www.nazarene.org/archives/index.html

Coats of Arms
(see Heraldry)

Colombia

www.world-newspapers.com
www.libdex.com/country.html
www.unicauca.edu.co/portafolio/archivo_historico/archivo_
    infogral.php
http://pilot.familysearch.org/recordsearch/start.html#p=0
www.familysearch.org

Comoros

www.world-newspapers.com
www.africa-research.org/mainframe.html

http://pilot.familysearch.org/recordsearch/start.html#p=0
www.familysearch.org

Congo

www.world-newspapers.com
www.africa-research.org/mainframe.html
http://pilot.familysearch.org/recordsearch/start.html#p=0
www.familysearch.org

Congo Democratic Republic

www.world-newspapers.com
www.africa-research.org/mainframe.html
http://pilot.familysearch.org/recordsearch/start.html#p=0
www.familysearch.org

Congregational

www.ucc.org/aboutus/archives/

Cook Islands

www.world-newspapers.com
http://pilot.familysearch.org/recordsearch/start.html#p=0
www.familysearch.org

Costa Rica

www.world-newspapers.com
www.libdex.com/country.html
www.archivonacional.go.cr

http://archivo.ucr.ac.cr
www.h-net.org/~latam/archives/project7.html
http://pilot.familysearch.org/recordsearch/start.html#p=0
www.familysearch.org

Côte d'Ivoire

www.world-newspapers.com
www.rootsweb.com/~jfuller/gen_mail_country-ivo.html
www.africa-research.org/mainframe.html
http://pilot.familysearch.org/recordsearch/start.html#p=0
www.familysearch.org

Crimea

www.huri.harvard.edu/abb_grimsted/index.html#Autonomous
www.huri.harvard.edu/abb_grimsted/O-2.html
www.archives.gov.ua/Eng/Archives
http://pilot.familysearch.org/recordsearch/start.html#p=0
www.familysearch.org

Croatia

www.libdex.com/country.html
www.rootsweb.com/~hrvwgw
www.riarhiv.hr/Default.asp
www.daz.hr/index.htm
www.arhiv.hr
www.carpatho-rusyn.org
http://pilot.familysearch.org/recordsearch/start.html#p=0
www.familysearch.org

Cuba

www.world-newspapers.com
www.cubagenweb.org/jaruco.htm
www.library.miami.edu/archives/intro.html
www.sanalejandro.cult.cu/pages/archivo/125.htm
www.arnac.cu
www.candoo.com/genresources
www.cubagenweb.org
http://pilot.familysearch.org/recordsearch/start.html#p=0
www.familysearch.org

Curaçao
(see Netherland Antilles)

Cyprus

www.libdex.com/country.html
www.heritage.org.cy/archives.htm
http://pilot.familysearch.org/recordsearch/start.html#p=0
www.familysearch.org

Czech Republic & Czechoslovakia

www.eegsociety.org/Index.html
www.libdex.com/country.html
www.nkp.cz/_en/pages/page.php3?page=orst_studovna2_
   en.htm
www.ahmp.cz/eng/index.html
http://archiv.pb.cz/Englindex.htm
www.mvcr.cz/archivy/eindex.htm
www.mvcr.cz/archivy/litomerice/english/index.html

www.cgsi.org
www.iabsi.com/gen/public
http://czechgenealogy.org
http://pilot.familysearch.org/recordsearch/start.html#p=0
www.familysearch.org

Denmark

www.world-newspapers.com
www.libdex.com/country.html
http://ddd.dda.dk/ddd_en.htm
www.infobel.com/world
www.aalborg.dk/serviceomraader/kultur+og+fritid/kultur/
    arkiver/default.htm
www.emiarch.dk/home.php3
www.dpc.dk/PolarLibrary/Start.html
www.grindstedbib.dk/arkiv/arkiv.htm
http://herningbib.dk/default.asp?id=15&mnu=15
www.sa.dk/lao
www.sa.dk/lav
www.sa.dk/lak
www.sa.dk/laa
http://holbo.dk/arkiv/default.php
www.2100lokalhistorisk.dk/Arkiv.htm
www.ringe.dk/lokalarkiv
www.hab.de
www.censuslinks.com/index
www.genealogybranches.com/international.html
http://pilot.familysearch.org/recordsearch/start.html#p=0
www.familysearch.org

Disciples of Christ (see Christian Church)

Djibouti

www.world-newspapers.com
www.africa-research.org/mainframe.html
http://pilot.familysearch.org/recordsearch/start.html#p=0
www.familysearch.org

Dominica

www.world-newspapers.com
www.candoo.com/genresources
www.candoo.com/genresources/dominica.htm
http://pilot.familysearch.org/recordsearch/start.html#p=0
www.familysearch.org

Dominican Republic

www.world-newspapers.com
www.libdex.com/country.html
www.candoo.com/genresources
www.rootsweb.com/~domwgw/mhhbcgw.htm
http://pilot.familysearch.org/recordsearch/start.html#p=0
www.familysearch.org

Doukhobors

www.saskgenealogy.com/cemetery/cem_religion.asp
www.doukhobor.org
http://edocs.lib.sfu.ca/projects/Doukhobor-Collection

East Galicia (Ukraine)

www.eegsociety.org/Index.html
http://pilot.familysearch.org/recordsearch/start.html#p=0
www.familysearch.org

East Prussia

www.eegsociety.org/Index.html
http://pilot.familysearch.org/recordsearch/start.html#p=0
www.familysearch.org

East Timor

www.world-newspapers.com
http://pilot.familysearch.org/recordsearch/start.html#p=0
www.familysearch.org

Easter Island

www.netaxs.com/~trance/rapanui.html
www.rootsweb.com/~pyfwgw/easter/ea-tr.htm
http://pilot.familysearch.org/recordsearch/start.html#p=0
www.familysearch.org

Ecuador

www.world-newspapers.com
www.libdex.com/country.html
www.ane.gov.ec/ane/site/welcome.htm
www.h-net.org/~latam/archives/archivo-municipal-camilo.html
www.h-net.org/~latam/archives/archivo-ecuador.html

www.h-net.org/~latam/archives/archivo-guayas.html
http://pilot.familysearch.org/recordsearch/start.html#p=0
www.familysearch.org

Egypt

www.world-newspapers.com
www.uq.net.au/~zzhsoszy/files/gg_index.html
www.libdex.com/country.html
http://pilot.familysearch.org/recordsearch/start.html#p=0
www.familysearch.org
http://lib.aucegypt.edu/screens/rbscl.html
www.africa-research.org/mainframe.html

Ekaterinoslav

www.eegsociety.org/Index.html
http://pilot.familysearch.org/recordsearch/start.html#p=0
www.familysearch.org

El Salvador

www.world-newspapers.com
www.libdex.com/country.html
http://pilot.familysearch.org/recordsearch/start.html#p=0
www.familysearch.org

Ellice Islands
(see Tuvalu)

Emirates
(see United Arab Emirates)

England

http://www.pricegen.com/english_genealogy.html
http://www.familyrelatives.com:80/
www.cwgc.org/cwgcinternet/search.aspx
www.world-newspapers.com
www.findmypast.com
www.genuki.org.uk
www.1837online.com
http://www.durhamrecordsonline.com/
http://www.1901censusonline.com
http://pilot.familysearch.org/recordsearch/start.html#p=0
www.familysearch.org
www.britishorigins.com
www.nationalarchives.gov.uk
http://www.oldbaileyonline.org/
www.libdex.com/country.html
http://www.1851-unfilmed.org.uk/intro.htm
www.ancestry.co.uk
www.a2a.org.uk
www.oldbaileyonline.org
www.britannia.com/bios/azlist.html
http://freebmd.rootsweb.com/cgi/search.pl
www.camelotintl.com/tower_site/prisoners/index.html
www.infobel.com/world
www.ndad.nationalarchives.gov.uk
www.britishrecordsassociation.org.uk
www.burkes-peerage.net/sites/peerageandgentry/sitepages/
   home.asp
www.aim25.ac.uk
www.nationalarchives.gov.uk/hospitalrecords/
www.history.ac.uk

www.kcl.ac.uk/lhcma/misc/locreg.htm
www.m25lib.ac.uk
www.port.nmm.ac.uk
www.port.nmm.ac.uk/ROADS/subject-listing/hier/biog.html
www.archiveshub.ac.uk
www.mundus.ac.uk
www.cityoflondon.gov.uk/corporation/family-research
www.cityoflondon.gov.uk/corporation/family-research/
    registerSearchForm.asp
www.bl.uk/collections/orientaloffice.html
www.lambethpalacelibrary.org
www.brookes.ac.uk/services/library/speccoll.html
http://archive.guardian.co.uk/Default/Skins/DigitalArchive/
    Client.asp?Skin=DigitalArchive&enter=true&AppName=
    2&AW=1223761482937
www.rothschildarchive.org/ta/default.asp
www.rafmuseum.org.uk/london/collections/archive/index.cfm
www.royalsoc.ac.uk/page.asp?id=1684
www.britishorigins.com
www.ancestry.co.uk
http://freecen.rootsweb.com/
www.censuslinks.com/index
www.maxpages.com/poland/Census_Research
www.familyhistoryonline.net/database/index.shtml
www.railwayancestors.fsnet.co.uk
www.sog.org.uk
www.historicaldirectories.org/hd/findbylocation.asp
www.british-genealogy.com/index.html
www.familia.org.uk
www.lineages.com
www.familyrecords.gov.uk/topics.htm
www.yorkshirebmd.org.uk

Episcopal Church
(see also Anglican)
www.episcopalarchives.org/genealogy.html
www.lambuth.edu/academics/library/
    MemphisConferenceArchives.html
http://library.sewanee.edu/archives/index.html

Equatorial Guinea

www.world-newspapers.com
http://pilot.familysearch.org/recordsearch/start.html#p=0
www.familysearch.org

Eritrea

www.world-newspapers.com
www.libdex.com/country.html
http://denden.com/EritreanArchives/main.html
www.africa-research.org/mainframe.html
http://pilot.familysearch.org/recordsearch/start.html#p=0
www.familysearch.org

Essenes, Order of Nazorean

http://essenes.net/chronnaz.html

Estonia

http://www.isik.ee/
www.world-newspapers.com
www.libdex.com/country.html
www.genealoogia.ee

www.genealoogia.ee/English/fro.html
www.eha.ee/english/english.htm
http://pilot.familysearch.org/recordsearch/start.html#p=0
www.familysearch.org
www.folklore.ee/rl/era/ava.htm
www.kirmus.ee/Asutus/en/general.php
http://eja.pri.ee/
www.ra.ee/?topic=25
www.utlib.ee/en/index.php?cat=coll&name=rare

Ethiopia

www.world-newspapers.com
www.uq.net.au/~zzhsoszy/files/gg_index.html
www.libdex.com/country.html
www.africa-research.org/mainframe.html
http://pilot.familysearch.org/recordsearch/start.html#p=0
www.familysearch.org

Europe
(see specific country)

http://home.att.net/~Local_Catholic/#Select_Location
http://feefhs.org
http://pilot.familysearch.org/recordsearch/start.html#p=0
www.worldvitalrecords.com
www.familysearch.org

Falkland Islands

www.world-newspapers.com
http://pilot.familysearch.org/recordsearch/start.html#p=0
www.familysearch.org

Faroe Islands

www.libdex.com/country.html
www.sleipnir.fo/natarc.htm
http://pilot.familysearch.org/recordsearch/start.html#p=0
www.familysearch.org

Federated States of Micronesia
(see Micronesia)

Fiji

www.world-newspapers.com
www.uq.net.au/~zzhsoszy/files/gg_index.html
www.libdex.com/country.html
www.usp.ac.fj/library/collection/pacificcollection/pacific_
    collection.htm
www.janesoceania.com/oceania_genealogy
www.fiji.gov.fj
http://pilot.familysearch.org/recordsearch/start.html#p=0
www.familysearch.org

Finland

www.world-newspapers.com
http://my.tbaytel.net/bmartin/1901finn.htm
www.libdex.com/country.html
http://sfhs.eget.net/archives.html
www.lib.helsinki.fi/english/services/collections/specialcoll.htm
www.lib.helsinki.fi/english/services/collections/
    manuscriptcoll.htm
www.svenskacentralarkivet.fi

www.finlit.fi/english/kia/index.htm
www.finlit.fi/english/kra/index.htm
www.valtioneuvosto.fi/vn/liston/base.lsp?r=1121&k=
    en&old=754
www.tyark.fi/englanti.html
http://vesta.narc.fi/arkistolinkit
http://juoru.uta.fi/~otkike/heritage.html
http://pilot.familysearch.org/recordsearch/start.html#p=0
www.familysearch.org

France

www.world-newspapers.com
www.libdex.com/country.html
www.archivesnationales.culture.gouv.fr
http://www.stehelene.org
http://migranet.geneactes.org
www.geneactes.org/index-en.html
www.culture.gouv.fr/documentation/leonore/pres.htm
www.genealogy.tm.fr/acte.htm
http://les.guillotines.free.fr/
www.ancestry.fr
http://membres.lycos.fr/numa/assgensurnet.html
www.infobel.com/world
www.es-conseil.fr/pramona/liens.htm
www.france-genealogie.com
www.genefede.org/menu.php
www.notrefamille.com
www.v1.paris.fr/fr/culture/archives_paris/Ressources_
    documentaires/Archives_genealogiques.ASP
www.v1.paris.fr/fr/culture/archives_paris/Ressources_
    documentaires/Bibliotheque.ASP

www.frenchlines.com/recherche_fr.php
www.cdhf.net/fr
www.cdhf.net/fr/index.php?t=accueil&h=liens/cercles
http://www.archivesnationales.culture.gouv.fr/chan/index.html
www.france.diplomatie.fr/archives.gb
http://histoire-sociale.univ-paris1.fr/Document/Archives.htm
http://palissy.humana.univ-nantes.fr/labos/cht/fonds/index.htm
www.archivesnationales.culture.gouv.fr/camt
www.archivesnationales.culture.gouv.fr/chan
http://www.servicehistorique.sga.defense.gouv.fr
http://pilot.familysearch.org/recordsearch/start.html#p=0
www.familysearch.org
www.archives.uha.fr

Freemasons (Masons)

www.nymasoniclibrary.org

Friesland (see Netherlands)

Gabon

www.world-newspapers.com
www.libdex.com/country.html
www.africa-research.org/mainframe.html
http://pilot.familysearch.org/recordsearch/start.html#p=0
www.familysearch.org

Galicia, East (Ukraine) West (Poland)

www.eegsociety.org/Index.html
www.halgal.com

http://pilot.familysearch.org/recordsearch/start.html#p=0
www.familysearch.org
http://immigrantships.net/austria_poland_galicia1889.html

Gambia

www.world-newspapers.com
www.africa-research.org/mainframe.html
http://pilot.familysearch.org/recordsearch/start.html#p=0
www.familysearch.org

Georgia

www.world-newspapers.com
www.libdex.com/country.html
http://pilot.familysearch.org/recordsearch/start.html#p=0
www.familysearch.org

Germany

http://www.digento.de/titel/102564.html
www.eegsociety.org/Index.html
www.world-newspapers.com
www.libdex.com/country.html
http://freepages.genealogy.rootsweb.com/~fkruse/oldsports/
    index.html
www.heritagepursuit.com/Ellmendingen/Ellm.htm
http://membres.lycos.fr/numa/assgensurnet.html
www.odessa3.org/collections/families
http://pilot.familysearch.org/recordsearch/start.html#p=0
www.familysearch.org
www.ancestry.de

www.odessa3.org/collections/land/wprussia
http://sites.huji.ac.il/archives/GERMANY-LISTS/
Danzig%201.htm
www.libraries.uc.edu/libraries/arb/ger_americana/index.html
http://staufenberg.online-h.de/Archiv/index.html
www.gda.bayern.de/enp1.htm
www.gda.bayern.de/famfor.htm
www.eo-bamberg.de/eob/opencms/sites/bistum/seelsorge/
dioez_familie/index.html
www.ezab.de/e/ebframe.html
www.ekd.de
www.ekbo.de
www.bb-evangelisch.de/index.php?sid=2285
www.erzbistumberlin.de
www.archivzentrum.de
www.hdg.de/Final/eng/page426.htm
www.bundestag.de/htdocs_e/datab/index.html
www.evlka.de/archiv
www.lkan-elkb.de
www.lad-bw.de
www.landesarchiv-berlin.de/lab-neu/start.html
www.archiv-ekir.de
http://sites.huji.ac.il/archives
http://home.bawue.de/~hanacek/info/earchive.htm
www.archiverlp.de
www.francegenweb.org/archives.htm
www.dhi.waw.pl/en/biblioteka/nih/biblioteka
http://stevemorse.org/
www.censuslinks.com/index
www.maxpages.com/poland/Census_Research
www.volkerjarren.de
www.cgsi.org
www.baptisten.org/start/index.php

Ghana

www.uq.net.au/~zzhsoszy/files/gg_index.html
www.libdex.com/country.html
www.world-newspapers.com
www.africa-research.org/mainframe.html
http://pilot.familysearch.org/recordsearch/start.html#p=0
www.familysearch.org

Gibraltar

www.world-newspapers.com
http://pilot.familysearch.org/recordsearch/start.html#p=0
www.familysearch.org

Greece

www.world-newspapers.com
www.libdex.com/country.html
http://cmrs.osu.edu/rcmss/
http://pilot.familysearch.org/recordsearch/start.html#p=0
www.familysearch.org

Greek Catholic

www.halgal.com/halgal.asp

Greenland

www.libdex.com/country.html
www.rootsweb.com/~grlbalti/greenland.htm
www.geocities.com/Athens/9479/inuit.html

http://pandora.cii.wwu.edu/vajda/ea210/aleut.htm
http://pilot.familysearch.org/recordsearch/start.html#p=0
www.familysearch.org

Grenada

www.world-newspapers.com
www.candoo.com/genresources
http://pilot.familysearch.org/recordsearch/start.html#p=0
www.familysearch.org

Grodno

www.eegsociety.org/Index.html
www.archives.gov.by/EArh/E_Hist_grodno.htm
www.archives.gov.by/EArh/E_naz_ist.htm
http://pilot.familysearch.org/recordsearch/start.html#p=0
www.familysearch.org

Guam

www.libdex.com/country.html
http://vitalrec.com/gu.html
http://pilot.familysearch.org/recordsearch/start.html#p=0
www.familysearch.org

Guadeloupe

(see also Antilles Française)
(see also Martinique)

www.candoo.com/genresources

http://pilot.familysearch.org/recordsearch/start.html#p=0
www.familysearch.org

Guatemala

www.world-newspapers.com
www.libdex.com/country.html
www.hispanicsociety.org/english/library.htm
http://pilot.familysearch.org/recordsearch/start.html#p=0
www.familysearch.org

Guinea

www.world-newspapers.com
www.africa-research.org/mainframe.html
http://pilot.familysearch.org/recordsearch/start.html#p=0
www.familysearch.org

Guinea Bissau

www.world-newspapers.com
www.libdex.com/country.html
www.africa-research.org/mainframe.html
http://pilot.familysearch.org/recordsearch/start.html#p=0
www.familysearch.org

Guyana

www.world-newspapers.com
www.libdex.com/country.html
www.ghcaraibe.org
www.candoo.com/genresources

www.rootsweb.com/~guycigtr
http://pilot.familysearch.org/recordsearch/start.html#p=0
www.familysearch.org

Gypsy (Gypsies)

www.rtfhs.org.uk

Haiti

www.agh.qc.ca
www.world-newspapers.com
www.anhhaiti.org
www.agh.qc.ca/indexen.html
http://pages.infinit.net/cerame/heraldicamerica/etudes/
    haiti01.htm
http://pilot.familysearch.org/recordsearch/start.html#p=0
www.familysearch.org

Heraldry

www.heraldica.org
http://members.tripod.com/~GaryFelix/index1.htm
www.polishroots.com/herbarz/herbarz_index.htm
www.polishroots.com/heraldry/heraldry_intro.htm
www.polishroots.com/heraldry/russian_heraldry.htm
http://www.dig.com.pl/pther/
www.amateurheralds.org/
www.college-of-arms.gov.uk/
www.archives.gov.by/EItd/egenealogy.htm
www.polishroots.org/heraldry.htm
http://heraldiek.beginthier.nl/

http://namen.beginthier.nl/
www.stamboomsurfpagina.nl/regionaal.html
www.genealogy-heraldry.sk/
www.hagsoc.org.au/
http://uqconnect.net/~zzhsoszy/files/gg_index.html
www.geocities.com/SiliconValley/Garage/4464/Kamon1.html
www.genealogy-heraldry.sk
http://user.orbit.net.mt/fournier/mncop.htm
http://members.tripod.com/~GaryFelix/index5H.htm
www.archives.gov/research_room/genealogy/immigrant_
    arrivals/mexican_border_crossings.html

Hinduism (Hindu)

www.hinducouncil.com.au
www.swaminarayan.org
www.akshardham.com
www.gandhiserve.org/index.html

Holiness Churches
(see Pentecostal)

Holland (see Netherlands)

Honduras

www.world-newspapers.com
www.candoo.com/genresources
http://pilot.familysearch.org/recordsearch/start.html#p=0
www.familysearch.org

Hong Kong
(see China)

Hrvatska
(see Croatia)

Huguenots

http://huguenots-france.org/
www.b-efa.org/huguenotstreet/index.html
http://huguenots-france.org/english/normandie/caux/caux.htm
www.huguenot.netnation.com/general/
www.huguenotsocietyofamerica.org/
www.geocities.com/Heartland/Valley/8140/begin-e.htm

Hungary

www.rootsweb.com/~wghungar
www.natarch.hu/mol_e.htm
http://www.cookcountygenealogy.com/
www.bparchiv.hu
www.eegsociety.org/Index.html
www.world-newspapers.com
www.felix-game.ca
www.libdex.com/country.html
http://homepages.rootsweb.com/~andert/pomogy.htm
www.rootsweb.com/~wghungar
www.bparchiv.hu/
www.bacs-kiskun-leveltar.hu/e_index.html
www.c3.hu/~soparchv/
www.bogardi.com/cgi-bin/rdxlinks.pl?archives
http://pilot.familysearch.org/recordsearch/start.html#p=0

www.familysearch.org
www.vleveltar.gyor.hu/
www.nogradarchiv.hu/
www.szolarchiv.hu/jnsz_megyei_leveltar.htm
http://dav.hr/
www.vojvodina.com/kultura/html/archives.htm
www.archives.org.yu/amreza.htm
www.geocities.com/transylvania_archives_project/
www.c3.hu/%7Etolnalev/
www.c3.hu/%7Emev/tartalom/98_1_2/szebeni.htm
www.militaria.hu/
http://stevemorse.org/
www.gyormegy-arch.hu/
www.bekes-archiv.hu/
www.mek.iif.hu/porta/szint/tarsad/hadtud/adacta97/html/
    index.htm
www.hevesarchiv.hu/
www.th.hu/
www.bparchiv.hu/
www.bacs-kiskun-leveltar.hu/e_index.html
www.mol.gov.hu/
www.bogardi.com/gen/
leveltar.lap.hu/
www.mflsz.hu/fooldal/index.php?page=kiadvanyok/ei_
    leveltarak_ang.php
www.cimer.lap.hu/
www.mek.iif.hu/porta/szint/egyeb/lexikon/
www.pim.hu/
http://hungaria.org/hal/genealogia/index.php?&newsid=316
http://genealogia.lap.hu/
www.genealogy-heraldry.sk/
www.maxpages.com/poland/Census_Research

www.cgsi.org
www.iabsi.com/gen/public

Iceland

www.world-newspapers.com
www.libdex.com/country.html
www.inlofna.org/IABC/Welcome.html
www.kb.se/
www.archives.is/index.php?node=english
www.riksarkivet.no
www.ub.uio.no
www.ub.uu.se
www.hab.de
http://pilot.familysearch.org/recordsearch/start.html#p=0
www.familysearch.org
http://www.ra.se
http://rmc.library.cornell.edu/Fiske/

Ile Saint Jean
(see Canada, Prince Edward Island)

India

www.world-newspapers.com
www.uq.net.au/~zzhsoszy/files/gg_index.html
www.libdex.com/country.html
www.indialabourarchives.org
http://sycd.gov.in/archives/arch_about_eng.htm
http://kannadasiri.kar.nic.in/archives
www.kerala.gov.in/dept_archives/archid.htm
http://archivesmanipur.nic.in/introd.htm

http://nationalarchives.nic.in
http://pilot.familysearch.org/recordsearch/start.html#p=0
www.familysearch.org
www.nlindia.org/collection_rare_others.html
www.archive-india.org/folkland_contact.html
www.bl.uk/collections/orientaloffice.html
http://genealogy.about.com/cs/india/
http://genealogy.about.com/gi/dynamic/offsite.
    htm?site=http%3A%2F%2Fwww.ozemail.com.
    au%2F%7Eclday%2F

Indonesia

www.world-newspapers.com
www.uq.net.au/~zzhsoszy/files/gg_index.html
www.libdex.com/country.html
www.arsipjatim.go.id
www.anri.go.id
www.museeguimet.fr/gb/homes/home_id20407_u1l2.htm
www.rootsweb.com/~idnwgw
http://pilot.familysearch.org/recordsearch/start.html#p=0
www.familysearch.org
www.igv.nl/jir/jirnmgr.html

Inuit
(see also Nunavut under Canada)

www.nativeamericans.com/Inuit.htm
www.avataq.qc.ca
http://collections.ic.gc.ca/cape_dorset/index1.html
http://college.hmco.com/history/readerscomp/naind/html/na_
    011300_eskimo.htm

http://inuit.pail.ca
www.geocities.com/Athens/9479/inuit.html
www.islandnet.com/~jveinot/cghl/nunavut.html
www.fss.ulaval.ca/etudes-inuit-studies/volu22n1.HTML

Iran

www.world-newspapers.com/
www.uq.net.au/~zzhsoszy/files/gg_index.html
www.libdex.com/country.html
http://pilot.familysearch.org/recordsearch/start.html#p=0
www.familysearch.org
http://pages.ut.ac.ir/library/SALOONS.HTM#iran
http://en.wikipedia.org/wiki/Shah_of_Iran

Iraq

http://www.incia.co.uk/4667.html
www.world-newspapers.com/
http://al-rafidayn.cultureforum.net/history-heritage-
    philosophy-f9/iraqi-personalities-t580-30.htm#5671
www.uq.net.au/~zzhsoszy/files/gg_index.html
http://pilot.familysearch.org/recordsearch/start.html#p=0
www.familysearch.org

Ireland, Republic of
(see also Northern Ireland)

http://ifhf.brsgenealogy.com/
www.genuki.org.uk
www.libdex.com/country.html

http://griffiths.askaboutireland.ie:80/gv4/gv_family_search_
    form.php
www.ancestry.co.uk
www.goireland.com/genealogy/irish_famine.htm
www.infobel.com/world
http://pilot.familysearch.org/recordsearch/start.html#p=0
http://www.clarelibrary.ie/
www.familysearch.org
http://www.census.nationalarchives.ie/
www.tiara.ie
www.proni.gov.uk
www.nli.ie
www.ucd.ie/archives
www.rootsweb.com/%7Emiigsm
www.aihs.org/collections.html
www.nyu.edu/library/bobst/research/aia/
www.archives.ie/
www.genealogybranches.com/international.html
www.newirelandnb.ca/nb_irish_family_names.html
www.historicaldirectories.org/hd/findbylocation.asp
http://immigrantships.net/irish_arg/irish_arg1822_29.html
www.lineages.com
www.rootsweb.com/~irlkik/ihm/ire1841.htm
www.irish-roots.net
www.presbyterianireland.org/congregations/index.html

Islam

www.library.yale.edu/neareast/mss.html
www.friesian.com/islam.htm
www.forumancientcoins.com/historia/islam_gen3.htm
www.marashilibrary.com/english/bio-main.html#grand

Isle of Man

www.genuki.org.uk
www.ancestry.co.uk
www.isle-of-man.com/interests/genealogy/fhs
www.isle-of-man.com/interests/genealogy/sources.htm
www.historicaldirectories.org/hd/findbylocation.asp
http://pilot.familysearch.org/recordsearch/start.html#p=0
www.familysearch.org

Israel
(see also Judaism)

http://www.its-arolsen.org
www.world-newspapers.com
www.libdex.com/country.html
http://sites.huji.ac.il/archives/
http://jnul.huji.ac.il/eng/col_special.html
www.tau.ac.il/cenlib/eng/subLibraries/special_collections/
    collections.shtml
http://www1.yadvashem.org/about_yad/departments/archives/
    home_archive.html
www.cgil.milano.it/Archivio/
http://sites.huji.ac.il/archives/
www.amalnet.k12.il/sites/krazot/krai0012.htm
www.isragen.org.il
www.israelgenealogy.com/
http://pilot.familysearch.org/recordsearch/start.html#p=0
www.familysearch.org

Italy

www.world-newspapers.com
www.libdex.com/country.html
http://dpls.dacc.wisc.edu/Catasto/index.html
http://membres.lycos.fr/numa/assgensurnet.html
www.infobel.com/world/
http://www.rootsweb.ancestry.com/~itawgw/
http://www.rootsweb.ancestry.com/~itamolis/7lazio_index.html
http://www.rootsweb.ancestry.com/~itamolis/
http://members.aol.com/pointhompg/home.htm
http://www.italiangen.org/
http://www.angelfire.com/ok3/pearlsofwisdom/
http://www.trentinoheritage.com/
http://www.angelfire.com/mt/sicily1/
http://www.geocities.com/bigpomian/transat/intro.html
www.culturadimpresa.org/english/activi/Elenco_eng/
    elenchome_eng.htm
www.comune.fe.it/archivio/index.htm
www.regione.piemonte.it/cultura/archivi/index.htm
http://plain.unipv.it/
www.genealogylinks.net/europe/italy
http://pilot.familysearch.org/recordsearch/start.html#p=0
www.familysearch.org
www.anzwers.org/free/italiange
www.ancestry.it

Ivory Coast
(see Côte d'Ivoire)

www.world-newspapers.com
www.rootsweb.com/~jfuller/gen_mail_country-ivo.html

www.africa-research.org/mainframe.html
http://pilot.familysearch.org/recordsearch/start.html#p=0
www.familysearch.org

Jainism

www.jainsamaj.org
www.jainworld.com

Jamaica

www.world-newspapers.com
www.libdex.com/country.html
http://jard.gov.jm/main
www.mona.uwi.edu/records
www.genealogy-quest.com/collections/jamcens.html
http://users.pullman.com/mitchelm/jamaica.htm
http://jamaicanfamilysearch.com
www.rootsweb.com/~jamwgw/
http://genealogy.about.com/od/jamaica/
www.candoo.com/genresources/jamaica.htm
www.everygeneration.co.uk/familytree/donaldlindo.htm
www.rgd.gov.jm
http://pilot.familysearch.org/recordsearch/start.html#p=0
www.familysearch.org

Japan

www.digital.archives.go.jp/index_e.html
www.world-newspapers.com/
www.uq.net.au/~zzhsoszy/files/gg_index.html
www.libdex.com/country.html
www.rootsweb.com/~jpnwgw/

www.digital.archives.go.jp/data/index_e.html
www.archives.go.jp/index_e.html
http://abish.byui.edu/specialCollections/fhc/Japan/index.asp
www.library.utoronto.ca/east/
www.mofa.go.jp/about/hq/record/
www.archives.go.jp/
www.ndl.go.jp/en/service/tokyo/classic/index.html
www.pref.saitama.jp/A20/BA18/index1.html
www.pref.yamaguchi.jp/gyosei/common-files/sisetu/monjo/
    e4monjo.htm
www.museeguimet.fr/gb/homes/home_id20407_u1l2.htm
www.rootsweb.com/~jpnwgw/
http://abish.byui.edu/specialCollections/fhc/Japan/about.htm
http://pilot.familysearch.org/recordsearch/start.html#p=0
www.familysearch.org
www.stichting-sakura.nl
www.geocities.com/SiliconValley/Garage/4464/Kamon1.html

Java
(see also Indonesia)

www.uq.net.au/~zzhsoszy/files/gg_index.html
www.arsipjatim.go.id/
http://pilot.familysearch.org/recordsearch/start.html#p=0
www.familysearch.org

Jewish
(see Judaism)

Jordan

www.world-newspapers.com
www.uq.net.au/~zzhsoszy/files/gg_index.html

www.libdex.com/country.html
www.amman.edu/library.htm
http://pilot.familysearch.org/recordsearch/start.html#p=0
www.familysearch.org

Judaism

www.jewishgen.org
http://www.its-arolsen.org
www.eegsociety.org/Index.html
www.jgsgb.org.uk/downl2.shtml
www.cjc.ca/template.php?action=archives&Type=
   0&Language=EN
http://www.ikg-wien.at/static/unter/html/gs_index.htm
http://stevemorse.org/
www.isragen.org.il
www.bh.org.il
http://eja.pri.ee/
www.sephardim.com
www.jewishgen.org/Hungary
www.jewishgen.org/SAfrica
http://www.ushmm.org
http://www.yadvashem.org
http://www.ipn.gov.pl/wai/en/10/5
www.shtetlinks.jewishgen.org
http://geocities.com/winter_peter_4
www.nljewgen.org
www.jewishgen.org/sfbajgs
www.columbusjewishhistoricalsociety.org
www.jewishgen.org/jri-pl/jriplweb.htm
www.iajgs.org
www.rootsweb.com/~ukrodess/

www.rootsweb.com/~ukrodess/page3.html
www.orthohelp.com/geneal/egypt.HTM
http://sites.huji.ac.il/archives/page3.htm
http://sites.huji.ac.il/archives/wienna%20list.htm
http://sites.huji.ac.il/archives/GERMANY-LISTS/
    Danzig%201.htm
http://sites.huji.ac.il/archives/german%20collections.htm
www.orthohelp.com/geneal/differ.HTM
www.mygenealogy.ch/cemetery/
www.angelfire.com/al/AttardBezzinaLawrenc/
www.jgsgb.org.uk/snire.shtml
www.wiesenthal.com/site/pp.asp?c=fwLYKnN8LzH&b=242509
www.jhcwc.mb.ca/archives.htm
www.library.yale.edu/judaica/
www.ushmm.org/research/collections/
www.spertus.edu/collections_resources/index.php
www.rtrfoundation.org/
www.redcross.org/services/intl/holotrace/9-29-00.html
http://special.lib.umn.edu/umja/
www.jewishgen.org/jhscj/Archive.html
www.jhsmw.org/archives.html
www.cjh.org/academic
www.jtsa.edu/library/about/specialcoll.shtml
www.americanjewisharchives.org/aja/general/no_flash.html
www.jewishtoronto.net/content_display.html?ArticleID=58144
www.jewisharchives.net/
www.bibliomaven.com/judaica.html
http://mysql.snafu.de/cjudaicum/archiv/index.html
www.zetna.org.yu/zek/konyvek/43/repert.html
www.c3.hu/~bpjewmus/
http://sites.huji.ac.il/archives/
www.sephardim.org/jamgen/

www.bh.org.il/Genealogy/links.aspx#Algeria
www.jewfaq.org

Kampuchea
(see Cambodia)

Kazakhstan

www.world-newspapers.com
www.libdex.com/country.html
www.hartford-hwp.com/archives/53/index-b.html
http://pilot.familysearch.org/recordsearch/start.html#p=0
www.familysearch.org

Kenya

www.world-newspapers.com
www.libdex.com/country.html
www.africa-research.org/mainframe.html
http://pilot.familysearch.org/recordsearch/start.html#p=0
www.familysearch.org

Kherson

www.eegsociety.org/Index.html
www.lemko.org/genealogy/oblasts.html
http://pilot.familysearch.org/recordsearch/start.html#p=0
www.familysearch.org

Kiev

www.eegsociety.org/Index.html
www.archives.gov.ua/Eng/Archives/

http://www2.jewishgen.org/databases/vsia/vsiaweb.htm
http://pilot.familysearch.org/recordsearch/start.html#p=0
www.familysearch.org

Kirgizian

www.libdex.com/country.html
http://pilot.familysearch.org/recordsearch/start.html#p=0
www.familysearch.org

Kiribati

www.world-newspapers.com
www.janeresture.com/kiribati_genealogy
www.micronesiagenweb.com/islands/kiribati
http://pilot.familysearch.org/recordsearch/start.html#p=0
www.familysearch.org

Korea, North

www.world-newspapers.com/
www.uq.net.au/~zzhsoszy/files/gg_index.html
www.library.utoronto.ca/east
www.museeguimet.fr/gb/homes/home_id20407_u1l2.htm
http://pilot.familysearch.org/recordsearch/start.html#p=0
www.familysearch.org

Korea, South

www.world-newspapers.com/
www.uq.net.au/~zzhsoszy/files/gg_index.html
www.libdex.com/country.html
www.rootsweb.com/~korwgw-s/

www.library.utoronto.ca/east
http://archives.go.kr/e_gars/index.asp
http://library.snu.ac.kr/eng/use_infor/ancientdoc.jsp
www.museeguimet.fr/gb/homes/home_id20407_u1l2.htm
www.accessgenealogy.com/military/korean.php
www.lineages.co.uk/dwodp/index.php/World/Korean/
   %EC%82%AC%ED%9A%8C/
http://pilot.familysearch.org/recordsearch/start.html#p=0
www.familysearch.org

Kosovo

http://www.albanian.com/information/countries/kosova/
   index.html
www.rodoslovlje.com
http://pilot.familysearch.org/recordsearch/start.html#p=0
www.familysearch.org

Kuwait

www.world-newspapers.com
www.uq.net.au/~zzhsoszy/files/gg_index.html
www.libdex.com/country.html
www.rootsweb.com/~kwtwgw/
http://pilot.familysearch.org/recordsearch/start.html#p=0
www.familysearch.org

Kyrgyzstan

www.world-newspapers.com
www.libdex.com/country.html
http://countrystudies.us/kyrgyzstan/11.htm

http://pilot.familysearch.org/recordsearch/start.html#p=0
www.familysearch.org

Laos

www.world-newspapers.com
www.uq.net.au/~zzhsoszy/files/gg_index.html
www.rootsweb.com/~laowgw
http://pilot.familysearch.org/recordsearch/start.html#p=0
www.familysearch.org

Latin America
(see also by country name)

http://users.aol.com/mrosado007/address.htm
http://pilot.familysearch.org/recordsearch/start.html#p=0
www.familysearch.org

Latvia

www.world-newspapers.com
www.libdex.com/country.html
http://lists.rootsweb.com/index/intl/LVA/LVA-SALDUS.html
www.rootsweb.com/~lvawgw/
http://pilot.familysearch.org/recordsearch/start.html#p=0
www.familysearch.org

Lebanon

www.world-newspapers.com
www.libdex.com/country.html
www.can.gov.lb/index.html

www.rootsweb.com/~lbnwgw
http://genealogytoday.com/family/syrian/
http://pilot.familysearch.org/recordsearch/start.html#p=0
www.familysearch.org

Lesotho

www.world-newspapers.com
www.uq.net.au/~zzhsoszy/files/gg_index.html
www.libdex.com/country.html
www.rootsweb.com/~jfuller/gen_mail_country-les.
   html#AFR-LESOTHO
www.africa-research.org/mainframe.html
http://pilot.familysearch.org/recordsearch/start.html#p=0
www.familysearch.org

Liberia

www.world-newspapers.com
http://lists.rootsweb.com/index/intl/LBR/AFR-LIBERIA.html
http://ccharity.com/liberia
www.africa-research.org/mainframe.html
http://pilot.familysearch.org/recordsearch/start.html#p=0
www.familysearch.org

Libya
(Libyan Arab Republic)

www.world-newspapers.com
www.uq.net.au/~zzhsoszy/files/gg_index.html
www.libdex.com/country.html
http://lists.rootsweb.com/index/intl/LBY/AFR-LIBYA.html
www.africa-research.org/mainframe.html

http://pilot.familysearch.org/recordsearch/start.html#p=0
www.familysearch.org

Liechtenstein

www.world-newspapers.com
www.la.llv.li
www.llv.li/landesarchiv.li-redirect
www.genealogienetz.de/reg/CH/ver/sginfo-e.htm
www.genealogienetz.de/reg/CH/ver/grinfo-d.htm
http://lists.rootsweb.com/index/intl/LIE/LIECHTENSTEIN.html
www.nettyroyal.nl/link/liechtenstein2.html
http://pilot.familysearch.org/recordsearch/start.html#p=0
www.familysearch.org

Lithuania

www.world-newspapers.com
www.libdex.com/country.html
www.polishroots.com/heraldry/lith_rna.htm
www.inyourpocket.com/lithuania/vilnius/en/venue?id=
    LIVIENX00617Blt;3;333%7D
www.lithuaniangenealogy.org/
www.lnb.lt/
http://pilot.familysearch.org/recordsearch/start.html#p=0
www.familysearch.org
www.antiquesatoz.com/napoleon/lithtart.htm

Lutheran

www.lutheransonline.com/lutheransonline/genealogy
www.kinquest.com/genealogy/databases/marriages.html
www.odessa3.org/collections/churches

www.elcic.ca
www.lcceastdistrict.ca/malinsky.htm
www.lccarchives.ca
http://chi.lcms.org
www.ltsp.edu/krauth/archives.html

Luxembourg

www.world-newspapers.com
www.libdex.com/country.html
www.infobel.com/world
www.luxembourg.co.uk/genealog.html
www.editus.lu/accueil/index.php
www.roots.lu/Display.php?pagename=Page1
www.genealogylinks.net/europe/luxembourg
www.blue.lu/query?q=genealogy
www.stthomas.edu/libraries/special/LuxGenRes.htm
http://pilot.familysearch.org/recordsearch/start.html#p=0
www.familysearch.org
http://www.luxembourg.co.uk/genealog.html
http://www.dijkgraaf.org/benelux.htm

Macau (Macao)

www.libdex.com/country.html
www.icm.gov.mo/ICM/feinf.asp#ah
http://pilot.familysearch.org/recordsearch/start.html#p=0
www.familysearch.org
http://archiver.rootsweb.com/th/read/PORTUGAL/1998-05/
    0894718983

Macedonia

www.world-newspapers.com
www.libdex.com/country.html
www.albanian.com/information/countries/macedonia/index.html
www.rootsweb.com/~mkdwgw/
http://pilot.familysearch.org/recordsearch/start.html#p=0
www.familysearch.org

Madagascar

www.world-newspapers.com
www.uq.net.au/~zzhsoszy/files/gg_index.html
http://lists.rootsweb.com/index/intl/MDG/AFR-
    MADAGASCAR.html
www.africa-research.org/mainframe.html
http://pilot.familysearch.org/recordsearch/start.html#p=0
www.familysearch.org

Malawi

www.world-newspapers.com
www.libdex.com/country.html
http://chambo.sdnp.org.mw/ruleoflaw/archives/
www.rootsweb.com/~jfuller/gen_mail_country-mal.html
www.africa-research.org/mainframe.html
http://pilot.familysearch.org/recordsearch/start.html#p=0
www.familysearch.org

Mali

www.world-newspapers.com
http://lists.rootsweb.com/index/intl/MLI/AFR-MALI.html

www.africa-research.org/mainframe.html
http://pilot.familysearch.org/recordsearch/start.html#p=0
www.familysearch.org

Malaysia

www.world-newspapers.com
www.uq.net.au/~zzhsoszy/files/gg_index.html
www.libdex.com/country.html
www.keene.edu/library/OrangAsli/
http://pkukmweb.ukm.my/~library/special.htm
www.umlib.um.edu.my/ZABA.HTM
http://pilot.familysearch.org/recordsearch/start.html#p=0
www.familysearch.org

Maldives

www.world-newspapers.com
www.maldivesroyalfamily.com/maldives_china.shtml
www.ndl.go.jp/en/publication/cdnlao/034/3404.html
www.recipeland.com/encyclopaedia/index.php/Maldives
www.ndl.go.jp/en/publication/cdnlao/046/464.html
http://pilot.familysearch.org/recordsearch/start.html#p=0
www.familysearch.org

Malta

www.world-newspapers.com
www.libdex.com/country.html
www.angelfire.com/al/AttardBezzinaLawrenc
www.certifikati.gov.mt/?lng=mt
www.aragon10.free-online.co.uk/NotariesMalta.htm

www.aragon10.free-online.co.uk/NotariesGozo.htm
http://lists.rootsweb.com/index/intl/MLT/MALTA.html
http://pilot.familysearch.org/recordsearch/start.html#p=0
www.familysearch.org
http://en.wikipedia.org/wiki/Malta

Marshall Islands

www.world-newspapers.com
www.libdex.com/country.html
http://members.tripod.com/~alelemuseum/Archives.html
www.micronesiagenweb.com/islands/marshall
www.janesoceania.com/oceania_genealogy
http://pilot.familysearch.org/recordsearch/start.html#p=0
www.familysearch.org

Martinique
(see also Antilles Françaises)

www.candoo.com/genresources
http://pilot.familysearch.org/recordsearch/start.html#p=0
www.familysearch.org

Masons
(also see Freemasons)

www.nymasoniclibrary.org

Mauritania

www.world-newspapers.com
www.libdex.com/country.html

http://lists.rootsweb.com/index/intl/MRT/AFR-
    MAURITANIA.html
www.thenationofmoorish-americans.org/golden01.htm
www.africa-research.org/mainframe.html
http://pilot.familysearch.org/recordsearch/start.html#p=0
www.familysearch.org

Mauritius

www.world-newspapers.com
www.libdex.com/country.html
www.uom.ac.mu/Library/library.htm#coll
www.cousinconnect.com/p/a/113/
http://lists.rootsweb.com/index/intl/MUS/AFR-
    MAURITIUS.html
www.africa-research.org/mainframe.html
http://pilot.familysearch.org/recordsearch/start.html#p=0
www.familysearch.org

Mennonite

www.eegsociety.org/Index.html
http://www.mcusa-archives.org/
www.mennonites.ca/canada.html
www.mcusa-archives.org
www.mhsc.ca/index.html
www.mhsc.ca
www.mcusa-archives.org
www.goshen.edu/mhl
www.lmhs.org/archive/index.html
www.mhep.org/library.html
www.emu.edu/library/histlib.html

www.maxpages.com/poland/Census_Research
http://feefhs.org/MEN/indexmen.html
http://members.aol.com/rhin0/genealogy.html

Methodists

www.depts.drew.edu/lib/uma.html
www.gcah.org
http://go.owu.edu/~librweb/spuma.htm
http://library.owu.edu/spuma.htm
www.lycoming.edu/umarch/
www.wofford.edu/sandorTeszlerLibrary/archives/default.asp
www.lambuth.edu/academics/library/
    MemphisConferenceArchives.html
www.gcah.org/Searching.htm

Métis

www.othermetis.net/AboGene/genelink.html
www.rootsweb.com/~wioconto/Lakesfamilies.htm#martell2
http://members.aol.com/vwilson577/1836-mix.html
www.lexisnexis.com/academic/guides/western_hist/
    st_louis_fur/fur12.asp
www.metisresourcecentre.mb.ca/genealogy
www.nativeamericans.com/Metis.htm
www.rootsweb.com/~cansk/Saskatchewan/ethnic/
    metis-saskatchewan.html
www.rootsweb.com/~nametis
www.glenbow.org/collections/archives/genealogy
www.quintinpublications.com/metis.htm
www.native-languages.org/metis.htm
www.metisduquebec.ca/genealogie.htm

Mexico

http://pilot.familysearch.org/recordsearch/start.html#p=0
www.familysearch.org
www.world-newspapers.com
www.libdex.com/country.html
http://home.att.net/~Local_Catholic/#Select_Location
http://members.tripod.com/~GaryFelix/index1.htm
www.infobel.com/teldir/default.asp
www.hispanicsociety.org/english/library.htm
www.agn.gob.mx/
http://aham.arquidiocesismexico.org.mx/
www.bibliog.unam.mx/bib/colecciones/fondosec2.html
www.bibliog.unam.mx/bib/colecciones/fondosec1.html
http://biblio.colmex.mx/info/colgral.htm#f
www.bib.uia.mx/colecciones/doc/acervos_historicos.html
www.h-net.org/~latam/archives/archivo-chiapas.pdf
www.h-net.org/~latam/archives/project5.html
www.h-net.org/~latam/archives/project4.html
www.h-net.org/~latam/archives/project2.html
www.h-net.org/~latam/archives/project1.html
www.h-net.org/~latam/archives/archivo-his-mil.html
www.h-net.org/~latam/archives/project6.html
www.h-net.org/~latam/archives/project9.html
www.h-net.org/~latam/archives/merida.html
www.censuslinks.com/index
www.rootsweb.com/~mexwgw
http://members.aol.com/mrosado007/mxcivreg.htm
http://members.tripod.com/~GaryFelix/index5H.htm
www.familysearch.org

Micronesia

www.world-newspapers.com
www.micronesiagenweb.com
www.fsmgov.org/birth.html
http://pilot.familysearch.org/recordsearch/start.html#p=0
www.familysearch.org

Minsk
(see Belarus)

Moldova

www.world-newspapers.com
www.libdex.com/country.html
www.rootsweb.com/~mdawgw/
www.routestoroots.com/
www.rootsweb.com/~mdawgw
http://pilot.familysearch.org/recordsearch/start.html#p=0
www.familysearch.org

Monaco

www.nettyroyal.nl/link/monaco1.html
http://www.wargs.com/essays/lesbian.html
http://lists.rootsweb.com/index/surname/m/monaco.html
http://pilot.familysearch.org/recordsearch/start.html#p=0
www.familysearch.org

Mongolia

www.world-newspapers.com
http://userpage.fu-berlin.de/~corff/mfaq-3.html

www.msnbc.msn.com/id/5379014/
www.mongoliatoday.com/issue/5/
http://archaeology.about.com/library/atlas/blmongolia.htm
http://english.people.com.cn/english/200110/12/
    eng20011012_82128.html
www.smhric.org/E_Bulag_2.pdf
http://pilot.familysearch.org/recordsearch/start.html#p=0
www.familysearch.org

Montserrat

www.candoo.com/genresources
http://pilot.familysearch.org/recordsearch/start.html#p=0
www.familysearch.org

Moravia

www.eegsociety.org/Index.html
www.cgsi.org
http://czechgenealogy.org
http://home.bawue.de/~hanacek/egene/enrefov.htm
http://feefhs.org/CZS/frg-mohs.html
http://pilot.familysearch.org/recordsearch/start.html#p=0
www.familysearch.org

Moravian & Moravian Brethren

www.eegsociety.org/Index.html
www.enter.net/~smschlack/
www.moravianarchives.org/
www.moravianchurcharchives.org/
http://freepages.genealogy.rootsweb.com/~elainetmaddox/

Montenegro

www.albanian.com/information/countries/montenegro/
    index.html
www.montenegro.org
http://genforum.genealogy.com/montenegro
www.rootsweb.com/~mntwgw/
www.geocities.com/henrivanoene/royalmontenegro.html
www.rodoslovlje.com/phorum/read.php?5,1006
http://pilot.familysearch.org/recordsearch/start.html#p=0
www.familysearch.org

Mormons
(see Church of Jesus Christ of Latter-Day Saints)

Morocco

www.world-newspapers.com
www.uq.net.au/~zzhsoszy/files/gg_index.html
www.libdex.com/country.html
www.mygenealogy.ch/cemetery
http://lists.rootsweb.com/index/intl/MAR/AFR-
    MOROCCO.html
www.genealogie-gamt.org/index2.asp
www.africa-research.org/mainframe.html
http://pilot.familysearch.org/recordsearch/start.html#p=0
www.familysearch.org

Mozambique

www.world-newspapers.com
www.libdex.com/country.html

www.ahm.uem.mz/
http://lists.rootsweb.com/index/intl/MOZ/
    AFR-MOZAMBIQUE.html
www.africa-research.org/mainframe.html
http://pilot.familysearch.org/recordsearch/start.html#p=0
www.familysearch.org

Myanmar
(Burma)

www.world-newspapers.com
www.rootsweb.com/~mmrwgw/
http://pilot.familysearch.org/recordsearch/start.html#p=0
www.familysearch.org

Namibia

www.world-newspapers.com
www.libdex.com/country.html
http://millennium.fortunecity.com/hindmarsh/711/
    genealog/orte.htm
http://lists.rootsweb.com/index/intl/NAM/AFR-NAMIBIA.html
www.klausdierks.com/Biographies/Biographies_U.htm
www.africa-research.org/mainframe.html
http://pilot.familysearch.org/recordsearch/start.html#p=0
www.familysearch.org

Native Peoples
(Canada & U.S.A.)

www.gov.ns.ca/nsarm/virtual/mikmaq/
www.rootsweb.com/~usgwnar/

http://members.aol.com/bbbenge/front.html
http://digital.library.okstate.edu/kappler/index.htm
http://members.aol.com/esarrett/na/na_narc.htm
http://www.nsula.edu/creole/
www.rootsweb.com/~itgenweb/
www.windriverhistory.org/washakiearchi.html
http://anpa.ualr.edu/finding_aids/collection_finding_aids.htm
http://www.dar.org/library/speccol.cfm
www.marquette.edu/library/collections/archives/
    native_writes.html
www.gbl.indiana.edu/abstracts/gen5.html
http://library.vicu.utoronto.ca/special/jonesintro.htm
www.hamptonu.edu/museum/archives.htm
http://memory.loc.gov/ammem/
www.cr.nps.gov/aad/feature/feature.htm
www.cr.nps.gov/aad/feature/traveler.htm
www.censusfinder.com
www.nativeamericans.com

Native Peoples
(outside of Canada and U.S.A.)

www.anglican.org.nz/Resources/Archives1.htm
www.keene.edu/library/OrangAsli/
www.aiatsis.gov.au/lbry/cllctns/cllctns_hm.htm
www.cairnsmuseum.org.au/histsoc.html
www.library.uq.edu.au/fryer/index.phtml#special
www.library.unisa.edu.au/resources/collections/special.asp
www.usp.ac.fj/library/collection/pacificcollection/
    pacific_collection.htm
www.uog.edu/marc/collect.html
www.aucklandcitylibraries.com/general.aspx?ct=18

http://library.christchurch.org.nz/Central/AotearoaNZCentre/
www.natlib.govt.nz/en/using/2atl.html
www.presbyterian.org.nz/archives/archivesframe.html
www.library.auckland.ac.nz/subjects/nzp/nzphome.htm
http://library.canterbury.ac.nz/mb/genefich.shtml
www.waikato.ac.nz/library/resources/nzc/nzc_collection.shtml

Nauru

www.world-newspapers.com
www.micronesiagenweb.com/islands/nauru/
http://home.att.net/~Local_Catholic/Catholic-Australia-
    Oceania.htm#Nauru
http://pilot.familysearch.org/recordsearch/start.html#p=0
www.familysearch.org

Nepal

www.world-newspapers.com
www.uq.net.au/~zzhsoszy/files/gg_index.html
www.libdex.com/country.html
www.rootsweb.com/~nplwgw
www.museeguimet.fr/gb/homes/home_id20407_u1l2.htm
http://pilot.familysearch.org/recordsearch/start.html#p=0
www.familysearch.org

Netherland Antilles

www.libdex.com/country.html
www.ghcaraibe.org
www.candoo.com/genresources/nethantilles.htm
www.rootsweb.com/~antwgw

www.nationalarchives.an
http://spsearch.ilse.nl/searchresults.jspx?in=antillen
www.mavicanet.com/directory/eng/24164.html
www.candoo.com
http://pilot.familysearch.org/recordsearch/start.html#p=0
www.familysearch.org

Netherlands

www.world-newspapers.com
www.libdex.com/country.html
http://geneaknowhow.net/digi/resources.html
www.en.nationaalarchief.nl/default.asp
http://membres.lycos.fr/numa/assgensurnet.html
www.infobel.com/world
http://www.dijkgraaf.org/benelux.htm
http://archief.startpunt.nu/
www.archiefnet.nl/index.asp?taal=en
http://home.hccnet.nl/p.molema/archief.htm
http://archieven.beginthier.nl
http://home.hccnet.nl/jaw.warnar/brabant/
http://www.cbg.nl/
http://geneaknowhow.net/digi/resources.html
http://www.hope.edu/jointarchives/
http://www.historiekamer.nl/
http://www.stamboom.nu/forum/
http://www.xs4all.nl/~kvenjb/gennl.htm
http://familienamen.beginthier.nl
www.gencity.nl
www.stamboomsurfpagina.nl
www.linkhitlist.com/cgi/LHL_N.exe?G2L&LinkNo=918024
&ListNo=49837

www.swinx.net

http://genealogie.pagina.nl/

www.linkhitlist.com/cgi/LHL_N.exe?G2L&LinkNo=913612
&ListNo=49837

www.linkhitlist.com/cgi/LHL_N.exe?G2L&LinkNo=1107835
&ListNo=49837

www.linkhitlist.com/cgi/LHL_N.exe?G2L&LinkNo=911609
&ListNo=49837

www.voorouders.net/

www.drentsarchiefnet.nl/

www.archief.delft.nl

http://geneaknowhow.net/digi/resources.html

www.angelfire.com/ga/digit

www.stamboom.nu/forum

www.hennekam.org

www.genealogylinks.net/europe/netherlands

http://genealogy.about.com/library/authors/uchennekam2a.htm

www.ngv.nl

www.dutchgenealogy.com

www.euronet.nl/users/mnykerk/genealog.htm

http://pilot.familysearch.org/recordsearch/start.html#p=0

www.familysearch.org

Nevis
(see also St Kitts and Nevis)

www.candoo.com/genresources

http://pilot.familysearch.org/recordsearch/start.html#p=0

www.familysearch.org

New Caledonia

www.archives.gouv.nc
http://pilot.familysearch.org/recordsearch/start.html#p=0
www.familysearch.org

New Zealand

www.cwgc.org/cwgcinternet/search.aspx
www.nram.org.nz
www.natlib.govt.nz
www.archives.govt.nz/index.html
www.dnzb.govt.nz/dnzb
http://paperspast.natlib.govt.nz
http://freepages.genealogy.rootsweb.ancestry.com/~nzbound/
www.world-newspapers.com
www.uq.net.au/~zzhsoszy/files/gg_index.html
www.libdex.com/country.html
www.ccc.govt.nz/Handbook/archives.asp
http://library.christchurch.org.nz/Central/AotearoaNZCentre/
www.natlib.govt.nz/en/using/2atl.html
www.library.auckland.ac.nz/subjects/nzp/nzphome.htm
http://library.canterbury.ac.nz/mb/genefich.shtml
http://library.canterbury.ac.nz/services/collns.shtml
www.waikato.ac.nz/library/resources/nzc/nzc_collection.shtml
www.wellington.govt.nz/services/archives
www.wcl.govt.nz/wellington/heritageindex.html
http://pilot.familysearch.org/recordsearch/start.html#p=0
www.familysearch.org
www.nram.org.nz/
www.bl.uk/collections/oesoz.html
http://www.nzsghamilton.co.nz/

Nicaragua

www.world-newspapers.com
www.libdex.com/country.html
http://genforum.genealogy.com/nicaragua/
http://lists.rootsweb.com/index/intl/NIC/NICARAGUA.html
http://es.groups.yahoo.com/group/Gen_CentroAmerica/
www.rootsweb.com/~jfuller/gen_mail_country-nic.html
www.geocities.com/inghmiami/Genealogia_Nicaragua.html
http://pilot.familysearch.org/recordsearch/start.html#p=0
www.familysearch.org

Niger

www.world-newspapers.com
www.libdex.com/country.html
http://lists.rootsweb.com/index/intl/NER/AFR-NIGER.html
www.africa-research.org/mainframe.html
http://pilot.familysearch.org/recordsearch/start.html#p=0
www.familysearch.org

Nigeria

www.world-newspapers.com
www.uq.net.au/~zzhsoszy/files/gg_index.html
www.libdex.com/country.html
http://lists.rootsweb.com/index/intl/NGA/AFR-NIGERIA.html
www.theabi.org.uk/nigeria.htm
www.africa-research.org/mainframe.html
http://pilot.familysearch.org/recordsearch/start.html#p=0
www.familysearch.org

Nobility & Noble Families
(see Royalty & Nobility)

Northern Ireland

http://ifhf.brsgenealogy.com/
www.world-newspapers.com
www.libdex.com/country.html
www.groni.gov.uk/
www.aihs.org/collections.html
www.nyu.edu/library/bobst/research/aia
http://griffiths.askaboutireland.ie:80/gv4/gv_family_search_
    form.php
www.archives.ie/
http://www.census.nationalarchives.ie/
www.rascal.ac.uk/
www.genealogybranches.com/international.html
www.historicaldirectories.org/hd/findbylocation.asp
www.familia.org.uk
www.lineages.com
www.nireland.com/genealogy
www.nidex.com/genealogy.htm
www.rootsweb.com/~nirarm
www.rootsweb.com/~nirwgw
www.n-ireland.co.uk/pages/Genealogy
www.irishfamilyresearch.co.uk
http://immigrantships.net/irish_arg/irish_arg1822_29.html
www.proni.gov.uk
www.genuki.org.uk/big/irl
www.ireland.anglican.org/library/libroots.html
www.ireland.anglican.org/library/index.html
www.ancestryireland.co.uk

http://members.tripod.com/~Caryl_Williams/Eire-7.html
www.rootsweb.com/~irlkik/ihm/ire1841.htm
www.irish-roots.net
www.presbyterianireland.org/congregations/index.html
http://pilot.familysearch.org/recordsearch/start.html#p=0
www.familysearch.org

Norway

www.world-newspapers.com
www.libdex.com/country.html
www.rhd.uit.no/folketellinger/folketellinger_e.aspx
http://homepages.rootsweb.com/~norway/na2.html
www.naha.stolaf.edu/archives.htm
www.ub.uio.no/
http://ain.hibo.no/homepage/
http://sognogfjordane.kulturnett.no/arkivnett/heimeside.htm
www.bergen.kommune.no/byarkivet/
http://sognogfjordane.kulturnett.no/arkivnett/kommunar/
    vik/lokhistarkiv.htm
www.ub.ntnu.no/
www.ub.uib.no/avdeling/spes/manuskript/manuskriptindex.htm
www.byarkivet.oslo.kommune.no/
www.farkiv.ol.no/
www.a-arkiv.telemarksnett.no/
www.arbark.no/
http://folk.uio.no/achristo/index.html
http://www.geocities.com/Heartland/3856/
http://www.nndata.no/home/jborgos/jborgose.htm
http://www.fellesraad.com/
http://www.geocities.com/genealogyno/
http://www.geocities.com/coastwater/nina_moller_nordby.html

www.censusfinder.com
www.censuslinks.com/index
www.genealogybranches.com/international.html
http://www.rootsweb.com/~wgnorway/
http://pilot.familysearch.org/recordsearch/start.html#p=0
www.familysearch.org
www.norway-genealogy.com
www.utvandrersenteret.no

Oceania

http://home.att.net/~Local_Catholic/#Select_Location
www.janesoceania.com/oceania_genealogy
www.haabaa.com/dir/323/13.php
www.rootsweb.com/~pacifgw
http://pilot.familysearch.org/recordsearch/start.html#p=0
www.familysearch.org

Oman

www.world-newspapers.com
www.uq.net.au/~zzhsoszy/files/gg_index.html
www.libdex.com/country.html
www.forumancientcoins.com/historia/islam_gen5.htm
http://pilot.familysearch.org/recordsearch/start.html#p=0
www.familysearch.org

Ottoman Empire
*(see Turkey, Greece, Palestine, Syria, Libya, Egypt,
Hungary, Yugoslavia, Croatia, Bosnia, Albania, Macedonia,
Romania, Moldova, Bulgaria, southern Ukraine, Turkey,
Georgia, Armenia, Iraq, Kuwait, Cyprus, Lebanon, Jordan,*

Eastern and Western Saudi Arabia, Oman, Bahrain, eastern Yemen, Egypt, Tunisia, and northern Algeria)

www.geocities.com/EnchantedForest/1321/index.html
http://pilot.familysearch.org/recordsearch/start.html#p=0
www.familysearch.org

Pacific
(see also Oceania)

www.bl.uk/collections/asiapacificafrica.html
http://rspas.anu.edu.au/pambu
http://pilot.familysearch.org/recordsearch/start.html#p=0
www.familysearch.org

Pakistan

www.world-newspapers.com
www.libdex.com/country.html
www.geocities.com/rabiazafar78/pakgenweb.html
www.museeguimet.fr/gb/homes/home_id20407_u1l2.htm
www.rootsweb.com/~jfuller/gen_mail_country-pak.html
http://members.ozemail.com.au/~clday/
http://pilot.familysearch.org/recordsearch/start.html#p=0
www.familysearch.org

Palau

www.world-newspapers.com
www.micronesiagenweb.com/islands/palau
www.janesoceania.com/oceania_genealogy
http://pilot.familysearch.org/recordsearch/start.html#p=0
www.familysearch.org

Palestine

www.world-newspapers.com
www.libdex.com/country.html
www.isragen.org.il/ROS/namechanges.html
http://pilot.familysearch.org/recordsearch/start.html#p=0
www.familysearch.org

Palitinate (Palitines)

http://www.palam.org/bkstore3/
http://members.aol.com/ntgen/taylor/palatine.html
www.rootsweb.com/~ote/palatines

Panama

www.world-newspapers.com
www.libdex.com/country.html
www.rootsweb.com/~jfuller/gen_mail_country-pan.html
http://users.aol.com/mrosado007/address.htm
http://pilot.familysearch.org/recordsearch/start.html#p=0
www.familysearch.org

Papua New Guinea

www.world-newspapers.com
http://lists.rootsweb.com/index/intl/PNG/
    PAPUA-NEWGUINEA.html
http://freepages.genealogy.rootsweb.com/~arkbios/png/
http://coombs.anu.edu.au/SpecialProj/PNG/Index.htm
http://pilot.familysearch.org/recordsearch/start.html#p=0
www.familysearch.org

Paraguay

www.world-newspapers.com
http://www1.lanic.utexas.edu/la/sa/paraguay/
www.pyadopt.org
www.gencircles.com/clubs/world/paraguay
www.bvp.org.py/index.htm
www.guiaslatinas.com.py
http://es.groups.yahoo.com/group/ParaguayGenealogia/
http://pilot.familysearch.org/recordsearch/start.html#p=0
www.familysearch.org

Pentecostal Church

www.pctii.org/arc/general.html
www.agheritage.org/research/research.cfm
http://faculty.leeu.edu/~drc/

Persia
(see also Iran)

www.uq.net.au/~zzhsoszy/files/gg_index.html
www.friesian.com/iran.htm
www.therain.org/appendixes/app57.html
http://pilot.familysearch.org/recordsearch/start.html#p=0
www.familysearch.org

Peru

www.world-newspapers.com
www.libdex.com/country.html
www.hispanicsociety.org/english/library.htm

www.arzobispadodelima.org/iglesias/catedral/archivo.htm
www.bnp.gob.pe/index.htm
www.h-net.org/~latam/archives/archivo-arz-lima.html
www.h-net.org/~latam/archives/archivo-gen-lima.html
www.h-net.org/~latam/archives/project8.html
http://members.aol.com/mrosado007/peru.htm
http://genealogia.perucultural.org.pe/
www.bnp.gob.pe/index.htm
http://pilot.familysearch.org/recordsearch/start.html#p=0
www.familysearch.org

Philippines

www.world-newspapers.com
www.libdex.com/country.html
www.geocities.com/Heartland/Ranch/9121/
www.bibingka.com/names/default.htm
www.dlsu.edu.ph/library/archives/collections.asp
www.filipinaslibrary.org.ph/library/default.asp?id=Main%20
    Reference%20Library
www.geocities.com/Heartland/Ranch/9121/
www.census.gov.ph/data/civilreg/index.html
www.familysearch.org/Eng/Search/frameset_search.asp
http://revista.carayanpress.com/
http://pilot.familysearch.org/recordsearch/start.html#p=0
www.familysearch.org

Pitcairn & Norfolk Island

www.lareau.org/genweb.html
www.rootsweb.com/~ausnorfo
http://pilot.familysearch.org/recordsearch/start.html#p=0
www.familysearch.org

Poland

www.eegsociety.org/Index.html
www.world-newspapers.com
www.libdex.com/country.html
www.bkpan.poznan.pl/
www.poland.pl/archives/index.htm
http://linktoyourroots.hamburg.de/ltyr/Suchmaske/en/
    1,3825,,00.html
www.polishroots.com/herbarz/herbarz_index.htm
http://genealog.home.pl/
www.geocities.com/Athens/Olympus/8691/tpna.htm
www.odessa3.org/collections/land/poland/
www.odessa3.org/collections/land/wprussia/
www.archiwa.gov.pl/?CIDA=43
www.pgsm.org
www.gdansk.ap.gov.pl/english/linki/poland.php
www.piasa.org/polisharchives.html
www.archiwa.gov.pl/?CIDA=177
www.uni.wroc.pl/JEDNOSTKI/ARCHIW-E.HTM
www.maxpages.com/poland/Census_Research
www.halgal.com
www.mtu-net.ru/rrr/ukraine.htm
www.pgsa.org
www.polishroots.org/genpoland/
www.genealogylinks.net/europe/poland/
http://genealogy.about.com/od/poland/
http://slucki.republika.pl/
http://genealog.home.pl/
http://akuchinka10.tripod.com/polishgentranslate/
http://immigrantships.net/austria_poland_galicia1889.html
www.rootspoland.com

http://www.cookcountygenealogy.com/
www.jewishgen.org/jri-pl/
http://stevemorse.org/
http://pilot.familysearch.org/recordsearch/start.html#p=0
www.familysearch.org

Polynesia
(see also Tahiti)

www.anglican.org.nz/Resources/Archives1.htm
www.rootsweb.com/~pyfwgw/tahiti
www.rootsweb.com/~pyfwgw/frenchp/index.htm
www.janeresture.com/polynesia_myths
www.janeresture.com
http://philtar.ucsm.ac.uk/encyclopedia/poly/geness.html
http://pilot.familysearch.org/recordsearch/start.html#p=0
www.familysearch.org

Portugal

www.iantt.pt
www.world-newspapers.com
www.libdex.com/country.html
http://membres.lycos.fr/numa/assgensurnet.html
www.mygenealogy.ch/cemetery/
www.bn.pt/coleccoes/arquivos.html
http://www.geocities.com/fcandido2001/portgen/general.html
    cdi.upp.pt/
www.arquivo-madeira.org/
http://expertgenealogy.com/?x=SpainPortugalGen
http://www.lusaweb.com/
www.dholmes.com/rocha1.html

www.islandroutes.com/portgenart.shtml
http://home.att.net/~Local_Catholic/Catholic-Portugal.htm
www.well.com/user/ideamen/pgeneal.html
http://pilot.familysearch.org/recordsearch/start.html#p=0
www.familysearch.org

Posen

www.eegsociety.org/Index.html
www.posen-l.com
http://feefhs.org/indexger.html
www.polishroots.org/genpoland/pos.htm
www.jewishgen.org/InfoFiles/PosenResources.html
http://wiki.genealogy.net/index.php/Provinz_Posen
www.genealogienetz.de/reg/POS/posen_e.html
http://polishroots.netfirms.com/links/polish_archives.html
http://pilot.familysearch.org/recordsearch/start.html#p=0
www.familysearch.org

Presbyterian

www.presbyterian.org.nz/archives
www.pcanet.org/history
www.history.pcusa.org/index.html
www.presbyterian.org.nz/archives/archivesframe.html
www.presbyterianireland.org/congregations/index.html

Prussia

www.odessa3.org/collections/land/wprussia/
www.geocities.com/SiliconValley/Haven/1538/prussia.html
http://www.mennonitegenealogy.com/prussia/

http://carlnpat.customer.netspace.net.au/oefrr007.html
http://pilot.familysearch.org/recordsearch/start.html#p=0
www.familysearch.org

Puerto Rico

www.world-newspapers.com
www.libdex.com/country.html
www.icp.gobierno.pr/agp/
www.preb.com/geneal/ahasjpr.htm
www.preb.com/geneal2/adasj.htm
www.icp.gobierno.pr/bge/librosraros.htm
www.preb.com/apuntes6/iehjaa.htm
www.apellidositalianos.com.ar/archivos_puerto_rico.htm
www.rootsweb.com/~prwgw
www.sgarner349.com/Puerto_Rico
www.genealogiapr.com
www.vitalrec.com/pr.html
http://emt.web.prw.net/
www.pucpr.edu/biblioteca/index.htm
http://home.coqui.net/ciales15/index.htm
http://wp.pr.superpages.com/people.phtml
www.proyectosalonhogar.com/BiografiasPr
www.candoo.com
http://pilot.familysearch.org/recordsearch/start.html#p=0
www.familysearch.org

Qatar

www.world-newspapers.com
www.libdex.com/country.html
http://pilot.familysearch.org/recordsearch/start.html#p=0
www.familysearch.org

Qazaqstan
(see Kazakhstan)

Quakers

www.usgennet.org/usa/ny/county/dutchess/data/
    quakerindex.htm
www.swarthmore.edu/Library/friends
www.genealogy-quest.com/collections/nycquakers.html
http://plainfield.friend.googlepages.com/
www.interment.net/data/us/pa/york/warrington.htm
www.swarthmore.edu/Library/friends/
www.rootsweb.com/~engqfhs/
www.geocities.com/Heartland/Plains/2064/squaker.htm
www.rootsweb.com/~quakers
http://pilot.familysearch.org/recordsearch/start.html#p=0
www.familysearch.org

Reformed Church

www.rca.org/aboutus/archives/index.html

Republic of Ireland
(see Ireland & Northern Ireland)

www.world-newspapers.com
www.genuki.org.uk
http://pilot.familysearch.org/recordsearch/start.html#p=0
www.familysearch.org

Republic of the Marshall Islands
(see Marshall Islands)

Rhodesia, North
(see Zambia)

Rhodesia, South
(see Zimbabwe)

Romania

www.eegsociety.org/Index.html
www.world-newspapers.com
www.libdex.com/country.html
www.rootsweb.com/~romwgw/index.html
www.rootsweb.com/~romwgw/romaniaresearch.html
http://archives.unitarian.ro/
www.mae.ro/index.php?unde=doc&id=5045
www.maxpages.com/poland/Census_Research
www.genealogylinks.net/europe/romania
http://feefhs.org/RO/frg-ro.html
www.huntington.edu/srs/srsotherorganizations.htm
http://pilot.familysearch.org/recordsearch/start.html#p=0
www.familysearch.org

Royalty & Nobility

www.uq.net.au/~zzhsoszy/files/gg_index.html
www.4dw.net/royalark/
www.geocities.com/tfboettger/research/gergen.htm#G
ftp.cac.psu.edu/~saw/royal/royalgen.html
http://www.xs4all.nl/~kvenjb/gennl.htm
www.ac.wwu.edu/~stephan/Rulers/
www.angelfire.com/in/heinbruins/
www.xs4all.nl/~kvenjb/gennl.htm

http://pages.prodigy.net/ptheroff
www.royalist.info
www.geocities.com/christopherjbennett
www.tyndale.cam.ac.uk/Egypt/
www.heraldica.org/topics/france/roygenea.htm
www.nettyroyal.nl/link/genealogy.html
www.datarabia.com/royals/familytree.asp
www.britannia.com/history/monarchs/
wespatterson.com/biblical/gen.html
www.royalstuarts.org/
www.berkshirehistory.com/bios/index.html
www.polishroots.com/heraldry/lith_rna.htm
www.geocities.com/Tokyo/Temple/3953/
www.geocities.com/Athens/8420/main.html
www.janm.org/
http://gold.rajabhat.edu/eng/rbook.htm
www.burkes-peerage.net/sites/peerageandgentry/sitepages/
    home.asp
http://genealogia.lap.hu/
www.genealogics.org/prominent.php
www.genealogics.org/photohistory.php
www.genealogics.org/browsesources.php
www.agad.archiwa.gov.pl/eng/infoogeng.html
www.4dw.net/royalark/Persia/pahlavi2.htm
www.geocities.com/Tokyo/Temple/3953/
www.worldroots.com/brigitte/royal/royal00.htm
www.4dw.net/royalark/Korea/korea.htm
www.4dw.net/royalark/Laos/laos2.htm
www.casaimperial.org/principe.htm
www.nettyroyal.nl/link/monaco1.html
http://worldroots.com/brigitte/royal/sitemap2.htm

http://english.people.com.cn/english/200110/12/
eng20011012_82128.html

Russia

www.eegsociety.org/Index.html
www.world-newspapers.com
www.libdex.com/country.html
www.polishroots.com/heraldry/russian_heraldry.htm
www.rootsweb.com/~ruswgw/
www.mtu-net.ru/rrr/
www.iisg.nl/~abb/
www.odessa3.org/collections/families/
www.odessa3.org/collections/stpete/
http://cmrs.osu.edu/rcmss/
www.iisg.nl/~abb/
www.iisg.nl/~abb/rusfed.html
www.gasur.narod.ru/
http://hist.dcn-asu.ru/mcaa/
http://pandora.cii.wwu.edu/vajda/ea210/aleut.htm
www.genealogylinks.net/europe/germany/germans-from-
    russia.htm
http://pilot.familysearch.org/recordsearch/start.html#p=0
www.familysearch.org
http://stevemorse.org/

Russian Empire
(see country)

www.eegsociety.org/Index.html
http://pilot.familysearch.org/recordsearch/start.html#p=0
www.familysearch.org

Rusyn & Carpathian

www.carpatho-rusyn.org
www.cgsi.org
www.rusyn.com
www.tccweb.org
www.iarelative.com/slovaki2.htm
www.carpatho-rusyn.org/cra/petercra.htm
http://pilot.familysearch.org/recordsearch/start.html#p=0
www.familysearch.org

Rwanda

www.world-newspapers.com
http://webspinners.com/Gakondo/en/Lists/Genealogy.php
http://lists.rootsweb.com/index/intl/RWA/AFR-RWANDA.html
www.hrw.org/reports/1999/rwanda/Geno1-3-09.htm
www.africa-research.org/mainframe.html
http://pilot.familysearch.org/recordsearch/start.html#p=0
www.familysearch.org

Saint Kitts and Nevis
(see also Nevis)

www.world-newspapers.com
www.tc.umn.edu/~terre011/genhome.html
www.candoo.com/genresources/stknevang.htm
www.candoo.com
http://website.lineone.net/~stkittsnevis/
http://pilot.familysearch.org/recordsearch/start.html#p=0
www.familysearch.org

Saint Lucia

www.world-newspapers.com
www.candoo.com/genresources/historical.htm
http://users.aol.com/mrosado007/address.htm
http://home.att.net/~Local_Catholic/Catholic-CAmerica.htm
http://pilot.familysearch.org/recordsearch/start.html#p=0
www.familysearch.org

Saint Vincent and Grenadines

www.world-newspapers.com
http://sv.usaroots.com/
www.rootsweb.com/~vctwgw
www.hwcn.org/~aa462/svgref.html
www.candoo.com/genresources/historical.htm
http://pilot.familysearch.org/recordsearch/start.html#p=0
www.familysearch.org

Samoa

www.world-newspapers.com
www.uq.net.au/~zzhsoszy/files/gg_index.html
www.rootsweb.com/~samoawgw/index.html
http://pilot.familysearch.org/recordsearch/start.html#p=0
www.familysearch.org

Sao Tome and Principe

www.world-newspapers.com
http://lists.rootsweb.com/index/intl/STP/AFR-SAO-TOME-
    AND-PRINCIPE.html

http://archaeology.about.com/library/atlas/blsaotome.htm
www.africa-research.org/mainframe.html
http://pilot.familysearch.org/recordsearch/start.html#p=0
www.familysearch.org

Saudi Arabia

www.world-newspapers.com
www.libdex.com/country.html
http://lists.rootsweb.com/index/intl/SAU/SaudiArabia.html
http://workmall.com/wfb2001/saudi_arabia/saudi_arabia_
    history_nineteenth_century_arabia.html
www.angelfire.com/tn/BattlePride/Saudi.html
www.saudiembassy.net
www.saudiembassy.net/Country/History.asp
www.arabinfoseek.com/qatar.htm
http://pilot.familysearch.org/recordsearch/start.html#p=0
www.familysearch.org

Scotland

www.scotlandspeople.gov.uk/index.aspx
www.nationalarchives.gov.uk
www.world-newspapers.com
www.libdex.com/country.html
www.ancestry.co.uk
www.electricscotland.com/
www.medievalscotland.org/scotnames/
http://www.safhs.org.uk/
www.ffsq.qc.ca/
www.infobel.com/world
www.nas.gov.uk/

www.ancestry.co.uk
www.scan.org.uk/
www.angus.gov.uk/history/archives/Default.htm
www.gro-scotland.gov.uk/
www.gro-scotland.gov.uk/famrec/index.html
www.scotlandspeople.gov.uk/
www.historicaldirectories.org/hd/findbylocation.asp
www.familia.org.uk
www.lineages.com
http://pilot.familysearch.org/recordsearch/start.html#p=0
www.familysearch.org
http://comdir.bfree.on.ca/brantogs/
www.geo.ed.ac.uk/home/scotland/genealogy.html
www.familysearch.org/Eng/Search/frameset_search.asp
www.geo.ed.ac.uk/scotgaz
www.genuki.org.uk/big/sct
www.nls.uk
www.ktb.net/~dwills/scotref/13300-scottishreference.htm
www.anesfhs.org.uk
www.dgfhs.org.uk
www.gwsfhs.org.uk
www.lanarkshirefhs.org.uk
www.tayvalleyfhs.org.uk
www.cursiter.com

Senegal

www.world-newspapers.com
www.libdex.com/country.html
www.archivesdusenegal.sn/
http://lists.rootsweb.com/index/intl/SEN/AFR-SENEGAL.html
www.africa-research.org/mainframe.html

http://pilot.familysearch.org/recordsearch/start.html#p=0
www.familysearch.org

Serbia and Montenegro

www.world-newspapers.com
www.libdex.com/country.html
www.archives.org.yu/oarhivue.htm
www.arhiv.sv.gov.yu/e1000001.htm
www.archives.org.yu/amreza.htm
www.zetna.org.yu/zek/konyvek/43/repert.html
www.arhivpancevo.org.yu/arhive.htm
www.matf.bg.ac.yu/iak/
www.arhivzajecar.org.yu/
www.arhivns.co.yu/
www.yurope.com/org/tesla/arhive.htm
www.genealogylinks.net/europe/serbia-montenegro
www.geocities.com/henrivanoene/genserbia.html
www.chivalricorders.org/royalty/gotha/serbgen.htm
http://pilot.familysearch.org/recordsearch/start.html#p=0
www.familysearch.org

Seventh-day Adventist

www.andrews.edu/library/car/sdapiobits.html
www.andrews.edu/library/car/links.htm
www.avondale.edu.au/information/cooranbong/heritage.php

Seychelles

www.world-newspapers.com
http://freepages.misc.rootsweb.com/~barker/

http://smgf.org/demographics.html
www.africa-research.org/mainframe.html
http://pilot.familysearch.org/recordsearch/start.html#p=0
www.familysearch.org

Shintoism

www.sivanandadlshq.org/religions/shintoism.htm
www2.kokugakuin.ac.jp/ijcc/wp/bts

Siberia
(see also Russia)

http://pandora.cii.wwu.edu/vajda/ea210/aleut.htm
http://feefhs.org/maps/INDEXMAP.HTML
http://groups.yahoo.com/group/Kresy-Siberia/
http://pilot.familysearch.org/recordsearch/start.html#p=0
www.familysearch.org
http://stevemorse.org/

Sierra Leone

www.world-newspapers.com
http://lists.rootsweb.com/index/intl/SLE/AFR-SIERRA-
    LEONE.html
www.africa-research.org/mainframe.html
http://pilot.familysearch.org/recordsearch/start.html#p=0
www.familysearch.org

Sikhism

www.srigurugranthsahib.org

Silesia

www.eegsociety.org/Index.html
www.cgsi.org
http://freepages.genealogy.rootsweb.com/~elainetmaddox/
http://members.aol.com/BeallComp/silesia.htm
www.polishroots.org/genpoland/sil.htm
www.familysearch.org
www.genealogienetz.de/reg/SCI/sil-e.html
http://groups.msn.com/GermanGenealogy/silesiaschlesien.msnw
http://pilot.familysearch.org/recordsearch/start.html#p=0
www.familysearch.org

Singapore

www.world-newspapers.com
www.libdex.com/country.html
www.rootsweb.com/~sgpwgw
www.ecitizen.gov.sg
http://user.itl.net/~glen/asianintro.html
http://pilot.familysearch.org/recordsearch/start.html#p=0
www.familysearch.org

Slovakia

www.world-newspapers.com
www.eegsociety.org/Index.html
www.libdex.com/country.html
www.civil.gov.sk/SNARCHIV/uk.htm
www.rootsweb.com/~svkwgw/
www.tccweb.org
http://cmrs.osu.edu/rcmss/

http://src-home.slav.hokudai.ac.jp/library/lib-eng.html
www.genealogy-heraldry.sk/
www.nlr.ru:8101/eng/nlr/manuscript.html
www.nlr.ru:8101/eng/nlr/rbook.html
www.civil.gov.sk/SNARCHIV/uk.htm
www.archivneusohl.sk/
www.censuslinks.com/index
www.cgsi.org
http://www.iarelative.com/slovakia.htm
http://www.tccweb.org/
http://www.csagsi.org/
http://www.cgsi.org/
www.iabsi.com/gen/public
www.genealogy-heraldry.sk
www.iarelative.com/slovakia.htm
www.slovakia.org/society-geneology.htm
http://feefhs.org/iar/slovakia.html
www.geocities.com/familysk/research.html
http://pilot.familysearch.org/recordsearch/start.html#p=0
www.familysearch.org

Slovenia

www.world-newspapers.com
www.libdex.com/country.html
www.rootsweb.com/~svnwgw/index.htm
www.sloveniangenealogy.org/
www2.arnes.si/~rzjtopl/rod/drustvo/predst.htm
www.infobel.com/teldir/teldir.asp?page=/eng/euro/si
www.uidaho.edu/special-collections/euro2.html#si
www.angelfire.com/country/veneti/
www.gov.si/ars/1a.htm

http://www.carantha.net/
www.zal-lj.si/Ang/Ang.htm
www.pa-ng.si
www.pokarh-mb.si/index.php?id=2&L=2
www.pokarh-mb.si
http://pilot.familysearch.org/recordsearch/start.html#p=0
www.familysearch.org

Society of Friends
(see Quakers)

Solomon Islands

www.world-newspapers.com
www.rootsweb.com/~melwgw/solomons
www.janeresture.com/solhome/index.htm
http://dlc.dlib.indiana.edu/archive/00001487/
http://pilot.familysearch.org/recordsearch/start.html#p=0
www.familysearch.org

Somalia

www.world-newspapers.com
www.libdex.com/country.html
lists.rootsweb.com/index/intl/SOM/AFR-SOMALIA.html
http://countrystudies.us/somalia/4.htm
http://www.somaliawatch.org/archivefeb01/010312201.htm
http://countrystudies.us/somalia/38.htm
www.africa-research.org/mainframe.html
http://pilot.familysearch.org/recordsearch/start.html#p=0
www.familysearch.org

South Africa

www.national.archsrch.gov.za/sm300cv/smws/sm300dl
www.ggsa.info
www.cwgc.org/cwgcinternet/search.aspx
http://rapidttp.com/milhist/
www.national.archives.gov.za/
http://home.global.co.za/~mercon/index.htm
www.world-newspapers.com
www.libdex.com/country.html
www.library.unp.ac.za/paton/collections.htm
www.brenthurst.org.za/library.htm
http://home.att.net/~Local_Catholic/#Select_Location
www.national.archives.gov.za/
www.nlsa.ac.za/collections_special.html
www.puk.ac.za/biblioteek/about_e.html#SpecialCollections
www.rhodes.ac.za/library/cory/index.html
www.wits.ac.za/saha/
www.lib.uct.ac.za/rarebks/
www.lib.uct.ac.za/rarebks/index.php?html=/rarebks/
    collections.htm&id=193&libid=29
www.unisa.ac.za/Default.asp?Cmd=ViewContent&
    ContentID=7160
www.sun.ac.za/library/eng/about/Collections/
    SpecialCollections.html#africana
www.national.archives.gov.za/dir_repository1999.htm
www.jewishgen.org/infofiles/za-infoa.txt
www.geocities.com/Heartland/Meadows/7589/genea_en.html
www.genealogy.co.za
http://lists.rootsweb.com/index/intl/ZAF/SOUTH-AFRICA.html
http://genealogy.about.com/od/south_africa
www.hagsoc.org.au/sagraves/index.php

www.africagenweb.org
www.1820settlers.com
http://home.global.co.za/~mercon
www.familysearch.org
www.africa-research.org/mainframe.html
http://pilot.familysearch.org/recordsearch/start.html#p=0
www.familysearch.org

Spain

www.world-newspapers.com
http://www.uclm.es/archivo
www.irargi.org
http://membres.lycos.fr/numa/assgensurnet.html
www.libdex.com/country.html
www.infobel.com/world
www.mcu.es/
www.usc.es/~troia/paleo/arquivos.html
www.xtec.es/~aguiu1/socials/arxius.htm
www.xtec.es/~aguiu1/socials/museus.htm
www.arxivers.com/cat/links.asp
www.usc.es/arquivo/
www.bib.ub.es/www7/7res1.htm
www.irargi.org/02default.htm
www.genealogia-es.com
www.genealogia-es.com/enlazarc.html
www.worldgenweb.org
http://members.aol.com/balboanet/spain/chart.html
www.rootsweb.com/~espandal
http://www.geocities.com/genealogiacanaria/
www.spanish-genealogy.com
http://pilot.familysearch.org/recordsearch/start.html#p=0
www.familysearch.org

Sri Lanka

www.world-newspapers.com
www.libdex.com/country.html
www.rootsweb.com/~lkawgw/index2.html
www.familyhistory.laurieashton.com/srilanka.htm
http://users.bigpond.net.au/ceylondatabase/
www.defonseka.com/ancestry.htm
http://lakdiva.org/tennent/v1_p3_c01.html
http://web.pdx.edu/~mmlynch/srilanka/trip2002/background.htm
http://withanage.tripod.com/people.htm
www.lankalibrary.com/geo/dynasty.htm
http://pilot.familysearch.org/recordsearch/start.html#p=0
www.familysearch.org

Sudan

www.world-newspapers.com
http://lists.rootsweb.com/index/intl/SDN/AFR-SUDAN.html
www.meforum.org/article/22
http://bubl.ac.uk/link/s/sudan.htm
www.sudan101.com/people_groups.htm
http://vlib.iue.it/history/africa/sudan.html
www.lambethpalacelibrary.org/holdings/Guides/genealogy.html
www.msnbc.msn.com/id/5498149/
www.arabinfoseek.com/sudan.htm
www.africa-research.org/mainframe.html
http://pilot.familysearch.org/recordsearch/start.html#p=0
www.familysearch.org

Suriname

www.world-newspapers.com
http://vlib.iue.it/history/americas/Suriname/
www.surinaamsegenealogie.nl
www.jodensavanne.sr.org
www.nationsonline.org/oneworld/suriname.htm
http://pilot.familysearch.org/recordsearch/start.html#p=0
www.familysearch.org

Swaziland

www.world-newspapers.com
www.uq.net.au/~zzhsoszy/files/gg_index.html
www.libdex.com/country.html
www.gov.sz/home.asp?pid=2002
http://lists.rootsweb.com/index/intl/SWZ/
    AFR-SWAZILAND.html
http://freepages.genealogy.rootsweb.com/~royalty/africa/
    persons.html
www.royalty.nu/Africa/Swaziland.html
www.unpress.co.za/book.php?action=displaybook&conf%5B
    bookid%5D=57
www.africa-research.org/mainframe.html
http://pilot.familysearch.org/recordsearch/start.html#p=0
www.familysearch.org

Sweden

www.world-newspapers.com
www.libdex.com/country.html
www.foark.umu.se/census/Index.htm

http://membres.lycos.fr/numa/assgensurnet.html
www.genealogi.se/roots/
http://sfhs.eget.net/archives.html
www.augustana.edu/swenson/genealogy.html
www.americanswedishinst.org/archives.htm
www.genealogi.se
http://www.ssa.stockholm.se/
http://www.genhouse-sweden.com/sidor/indexe.html
http://www.sverigeatlas.se
www.arkion.se
http://www.algonet.se/~hogman/swe_genealogy.htm
www.ub.uu.se/
http://www.ra.se/
www.uppsala.se/uppsala/templates/StandardPage_____
    18293.aspx
www.foark.umu.se/english/search.htm
www.swemi.se/arkivet-12018.asp
www.raa.se/bibliotek/english/spec_coll.asp
www.ssa.stockholm.se/
www.norrtalje.se/templates/Page_____2534.aspx
www.norrkoping.se/kultur-fritid/stadsarkivet.xml
www.ra.se/kra/english.html
www.lund.se/templates/Page_____11817.aspx
www.linkoping.se/Organisation/Kommunstyrelsen/
    Arkivmyndigheten/index.htm
http://eskilstuna.se/templates/Page_____16264.aspx
www.ra.se/ula/english.html
www.censusfinder.com
www.censuslinks.com/index
www.genealogybranches.com/international.html
www.rootsweb.com/~swewgw
www.svar.ra.se

www.dis.se
www.foark.umu.se/census/Index.htm
www3.dcs.hull.ac.uk/genealogy/swedish
www.genealogi.se
www.abc.se/~m6921/geneal.html
www.inetmedia.nu/webbkarta
www.royalcourt.se
http://welcome.to/Elisabeth.Thorsell
www.genline.com/databasen/swedens_lan.php
www.augustana.edu/swenson
http://pilot.familysearch.org/recordsearch/start.html#p=0
www.familysearch.org

Switzerland

www.world-newspapers.com
www.fr.ch
www.libdex.com/country.html
www.eye.ch/swissgen/schweiz-en.html
http://www.eye.ch/swissgen/ver/bsinfo-e.htm
http://www.ghgrb.ch/
http://www.eye.ch/swissgen/ver/beinfo-e.htm
http://www.eye.ch/swissgen/ver/frinfo-e.htm
http://www.eye.ch/swissgen/ver/geinfo-e.htm
http://www.eye.ch/swissgen/ver/grinfo-d.htm
http://www.eye.ch/swissgen/ver/juinfo-e.htm
http://www.eye.ch/swissgen/ver/luinfo-e.htm
http://www.eye.ch/swissgen/ver/fpfinfo-d.htm
http://www.eye.ch/swissgen/ver/neinfo-e.htm
http://www.eye.ch/swissgen/GHGO/index.html
http://www.eye.ch/swissgen/ver/vsinfo-e.htm
http://www.eye.ch/swissgen/ver/vdinfo-e.htm

http://www.eye.ch/swissgen/ver/zhinfo-e.htm
http://www.eye.ch/swissgen/ver/tiinfo-e.htm
http://www.mindspring.com/~philipp/che.html
http://www.geocities.com/bigpomian/transat/intro.html
www.staluzern.ch/vsa/archive/archive.html
www.sozialarchiv.ch/
www.bundesarchiv.ch/bar/engine/Home
www.bundesarchiv.ch/bar/engine/ShowNewsWindow?lg=
    en_US#
www.ub.unibas.ch/wwz/wwzprosp.htm
www.stub.unibe.ch/index.php?p=1&i=70
www.ub.unibas.ch/info10h.htm
http://uniarchiv.unibe.ch/
www.zb.unizh.ch/index.html?http://www.zb.unizh.ch/
    sondersa/hands/brief.htm
www.eye.ch/swissgen
www.eye.ch/swissgen/verein-e.htm
www.genline.com/databasen
http://pilot.familysearch.org/recordsearch/start.html#p=0
www.familysearch.org

Syria

www.world-newspapers.com
www.rootsweb.com/~syrwgw
http://genealogytoday.com/family/syrian/
www.princeton.edu/~batke/itl/denise/abbasids.htm
www.finfo.dk/wwwfinfo/HTML/arabisk/Global_Links/
    Syrien.html
www.geocities.com/EnchantedForest/1321/index.html
www.tyndale.cam.ac.uk/Egypt/ptolemies/background/
    bg_daughters.htm

http://pilot.familysearch.org/recordsearch/start.html#p=0
www.familysearch.org

Tahiti
(see also Polynesia)

www.uq.net.au/~zzhsoszy/files/gg_index.html
www.anglican.org.nz/Resources/Archives1.htm
www.janeresture.com/polynesia_myths/tahiti.htm
http://berclo.net/page02/02en-tahiti.html
www.janesoceania.com/oceania_genealogy/
www.sacred-texts.com/pac/hhl/hhl13.htm
http://pilot.familysearch.org/recordsearch/start.html#p=0
www.familysearch.org

Taiwan

www.world-newspapers.com
www.libdex.com/country.html
www.rootsweb.com/~twnwgw/
www.msnbc.msn.com/id/8464488
http://ccs.ncl.edu.tw/conference_20041207/
    conference_03_19.htm
http://genealogy.about.com/library/authors/ucboey1a.htm
http://pilot.familysearch.org/recordsearch/start.html#p=0
www.familysearch.org

Tajikistan

www.world-newspapers.com
http://pilot.familysearch.org/recordsearch/start.html#p=0
www.familysearch.org

Tanganyika
(see Tanzania)

Tanzania
(United Republic of Tanzania)

www.world-newspapers.com
www.libdex.com/country.html
www.africa-research.org/mainframe.html
http://archaeology.about.com/library/atlas/bltanzania.htm
www.lib.utexas.edu/maps/islands_oceans_poles/zanzibar_
    island_76.jpg
http://pilot.familysearch.org/recordsearch/start.html#p=0
www.familysearch.org

Taoism (Tao)

www.abodetao.com
http://pilot.familysearch.org/recordsearch/start.html#p=0
www.familysearch.org

Thailand

www.world-newspapers.com
www.uq.net.au/~zzhsoszy/files/gg_index.html
www.libdex.com/country.html
www.rootsweb.com/~thawgw/
http://gold.rajabhat.edu/eng/lic.htm
http://gold.rajabhat.edu/eng/rbook.htm
http://library.tu.ac.th/detail/about.html#special
www.museeguimet.fr/gb/homes/home_id20407_u1l2.htm
http://pilot.familysearch.org/recordsearch/start.html#p=0
www.familysearch.org

Tibet
(see also Buddhism)

www.rootsweb.com/~tibetwgw/
www.museeguimet.fr/gb/homes/home_id20407_u1l2.htm
http://en.tibet.cn/en_index/hac/t20050701_39998.htm
www.tibet.com/Status/mongol.html
http://iris.lib.virginia.edu/tibet/xml/showEssay.php?xml=/
    collections/history/summaries.xml&l=d1e5588
http://ichhan.hp.infoseek.co.jp/list/tibete1.html
http://info.tibet.cn/en/culture/tis/t20050701_39763.htm
http://pilot.familysearch.org/recordsearch/start.html#p=0
www.familysearch.org

Timor

www.arsipjatim.go.id
www.clal.org/jpf1.html
www.suthlib.nsw.gov.au/ssc/suthlib.nsf/AllDocs/RWP3C6D40
    38DDB34AE9CA256E8C00355A96?OpenDocument
www.aph.gov.au/library/pubs/rp/2000-01/01RP21.htm
www.havenworks.com/world/east-timor
www.ess.uwe.ac.uk/Timor/background2.htm
www.cafod.org.uk/where_we_work/asia/east_timor/making_
    poverty_history_in_east_timor
http://pilot.familysearch.org/recordsearch/start.html#p=0
www.familysearch.org

Togo

www.world-newspapers.com
www.cia.gov/cia/publications/factbook/geos/to.html

www.infoplease.com/ipa/A0108038.html
http://lists.rootsweb.com/index/intl/TGO/AFR-TOGO.html
www.africa-research.org/mainframe.html
http://pilot.familysearch.org/recordsearch/start.html#p=0
www.familysearch.org

Tonga

www.world-newspapers.com
www.uq.net.au/~zzhsoszy/files/gg_index.html
http://freepages.genealogy.rootsweb.com/~royalty/tonga/
    persons.html
www.cousinconnect.com/p/a/174
www.nzetc.org/tm/scholarly/tei-TreMaor-b4-2-5.html
www.genealogy.org.nz/sig/pacific.html
www.janesoceania.com/oceania_genealogy
http://pilot.familysearch.org/recordsearch/start.html#p=0
www.familysearch.org

Transylvania

www.geocities.com/transylvania_archives_project/
http://archives.unitarian.ro/
www.transilvania.info/cgi-bin/indexing?AG_PROCESS=
    LISTSUBCAT&CAT=11&SUBCAT=150&FROM=
    0&LANG=1
www.genealogienetz.de/reg/ESE/7burg_info.html
http://feefhs.org/FIJ/DG-GSEE.HTML
www.bogardi.com/cgi-bin/rdxlinks.pl?regionalethnic
www.zum.de/whkmla/region/eceurope/xtransylvania.html
http://pilot.familysearch.org/recordsearch/start.html#p=0
www.familysearch.org

Trinidad and Tobago

www.world-newspapers.com
www.libdex.com/country.html
www.nalis.gov.tt/Heritage/Heritage.htm
www.mainlib.uwi.tt/wisc.html
www.rootsweb.com/~ttowgw
http://users.carib-link.net/~rfbarnes/
www.candoo.com/genresources/#TRINIDADTOBAGO
http://pilot.familysearch.org/recordsearch/start.html#p=0
www.familysearch.org

Tunisia

www.world-newspapers.com
www.uq.net.au/~zzhsoszy/files/gg_index.html
www.archives.nat.tn/eng/default.asp
www.genealogytoday.com/genealogy/planet.mv?Location=
    Tunisia&level=Country&gc=TUN
www.rootsweb.com/~jfuller/gen_mail_country-tun.html#
    AFR-TUNISIA
www.archives.nat.tn
http://archaeology.about.com/gi/dynamic/offsite.htm?
    site=http://www.northafrica.de/
http://archaeology.about.com/gi/dynamic/offsite.htm?
    site=http://www.northafrica.de/
www.genealogie-gamt.org/index2.asp
www.cousinconnect.com/p/a/176/
www.africa-research.org/mainframe.htm
http://pilot.familysearch.org/recordsearch/start.html#p=0
www.familysearch.org

Turkey

www.world-newspapers.com
www.uq.net.au/~zzhsoszy/files/gg_index.html
www.libdex.com/country.html
www.devletarsivleri.gov.tr/
www.archimac.org/Organizations/KEK.spml
www.archimac.org/Organizations/index.spml
www.muslimphilosophy.com/ik/klf.htm#FStT
www.sefarad.org/publication/lm/040/9.html
www.rootsweb.com/~turwgw
www.jewishgen.org/SefardSIG/izmir_infofile.HTM
www.mkutup.gov.t
http://pilot.familysearch.org/recordsearch/start.html#p=0
www.familysearch.org

Turkmenistan

www.world-newspapers.com
www.atlapedia.com/online/countries/turkmeni.htm
www.pupress.princeton.edu/chapters/i7858.html
www.econ.uiuc.edu/~slavrev/602abs.html
http://pilot.familysearch.org/recordsearch/start.html#p=0
www.familysearch.org

Turks and Caicos Islands

www.candoo.com
www.tcmuseum.org
http://users.aol.com/mrosado007/caicos.htm
www.tcmuseum.org/family_history_research/
http://pilot.familysearch.org/recordsearch/start.html#p=0
www.familysearch.org

Tuvalu

www.world-newspapers.com
www.tuvaluislands.com/history.htm
www.janeresture.com/about_tuvalu/tuvalu.htm
http://tuvalu.site.ne.jp/about/index.html
www.mapsouthpacific.com/tuvalu/index.html
http://en.wikipedia.org/wiki/Tuvalu
www.state.gov/r/pa/ei/bgn/16479.htm
www.janeresture.com/tuvalu2/home.htm
www.rootsweb.com/~pyfwgw/tuvalu/
www.frontlineonnet.com/fl1825/18250630.htm
http://islamic-world.net/countries/tuvalu.htm
www.cousinconnect.com/p/a/179/
http://pilot.familysearch.org/recordsearch/start.html#p=0
www.familysearch.org

Uganda

www.world-newspapers.com
www.uq.net.au/~zzhsoszy/files/gg_index.html
www.libdex.com/country.html
http://lists.rootsweb.com/index/intl/UGA/AFR-UGANDA.html
www.4dw.net/royalark/Uganda/buganda8.htm
http://home.att.net/~Local_Catholic/Catholic-Africa.htm#
    Uganda
http://us-africa.tripod.com/uganda2.html
www.myuganda.co.ug/about/history.php
http://pilot.familysearch.org/recordsearch/start.html#p=0
www.familysearch.org

Ukraine

www.eegsociety.org/Index.html
www.world-newspapers.com
www.libdex.com/country.html
www.huri.harvard.edu/abb_grimsted/index.html
www.huri.harvard.edu/abb_grimsted/index.html#state
www.rootsweb.com/~ukrwgw/index2.htm
www.halgal.com/
www.geocities.com/uggncr/
www.lemko.org/
www.tccweb.org
www.huri.harvard.edu/library.coll.html
www.genealogicaltree.org.ua/eng/eindex.html
www.archives.gov.ua/Eng/
www.huri.harvard.edu/abb_grimsted/index.html#Autonomous
www.huri.harvard.edu/abb_grimsted/
www.archives.gov.ua/Eng/Archives/
www.archives.gov.ua/Eng/genealogia.php
www.geocities.com/ukrainianfamilies/
www.halgal.com
www.mtu-net.ru/rrr/ukraine.htm
www.lemko.org/genealogy/oblasts.html
www.genealogylinks.net/europe/ukraine/
http://genealogy.iatp.org.ua/eng/othercountries/
http://pilot.familysearch.org/recordsearch/start.html#p=0
www.familysearch.org

United Arab Emirates

www.world-newspapers.com
www.uq.net.au/~zzhsoszy/files/gg_index.html

www.libdex.com/country.html
http://library.aus.ac.ae/services/more.html#special
http://genforum.genealogy.com/uae/
http://pilot.familysearch.org/recordsearch/start.html#p=0
www.familysearch.org

United Church of Canada

www.rootsweb.com/~canns/united.html
http://www.united-church.ca/local/archives
http://unitedchurcharchives.vicu.utoronto.ca/

United Kingdom
(see component countries)

www.nationalarchives.gov.uk
www.familysearch.org
www.cwgc.org/cwgcinternet/search.aspx
www.findmypast.com
ancestry.uk
www.infobel.com/world
www.genealogybranches.com/international.html
www.genuki.org.uk
www.uk-genealogy.org.uk
http://pilot.familysearch.org/recordsearch/start.html#p=0
www.familysearch.org
http://ancestry.co.uk

United States of America
(First, this list shows websites that are USA-wide. Following this list, see also each State listed separately)

http://pilot.familysearch.org/recordsearch/start.html#p=0
www.familysearch.org
www.archives.gov/research_room/genealogy
GenealogyBank.com
www.footnote.com
http://www.godfrey.org./
PeopleFinders.com
www.world-newspapers.com
www.newenglandancestors.org
www.afrigeneas.com
www.libdex.com/country.html
http://www.ellisisland.org/search/passSearch.asp
http://home.att.net/~Local_Catholic/#Select_Location
www.virtualjamestown.org/servantcontracts.html
http://home.att.net/~wee-monster/military.html
www.worldvitalrecords.com
www.loc.gov/rr/
www.usgenweb.org/
www.ancestry.com
www.genealogy.com
www.acpl.lib.in.us/genealogy/persi.html
www.kindredkonnections.com
www.francoamericancentrenh.com/
http://stevemorse.org/
www.uidaho.edu/special-
    collections/Other.Repositories.html
www.americanantiquarian.org/digital2.htm
http://special.lib.umn.edu/ymca/
www.archives.gov/facilities/mo/st_louis.html
www.digital-librarian.com/genealogy.html
www.circusworldmuseum.com/library/research.html
www.ellisislandrecords.org

www.hunterinformation.com/corporat.htm
www.astro.uni-bonn.de/~pbrosche/hist_sci/hs_arch.html
http://mla-hhss.org/histloca.htm
http://www.onegreatfamily.com/Home.aspx
http://www.lib.byu.edu/subsutility/index.php?sid=16
www.sharpweb.org/
http://scriptorium.lib.duke.edu/women/article.html
www.hunterinformation.com/corporat.htm
www.heritagequestonline.com
http://www.gengateway.com/american_genealogy.htm
www.census-online.com/links/United_States/
CriminalSearches.com
Intelius.com
Peoplescanner.com
www.lineages.com

United States (by State)

Alabama

www.rootsweb.com/roots-l/USA/al.html
www.algenweb.us
GenealogyBank.com
http://www.archives.state.al.us/ge.html
www.interment.net/us/al/index.htm
www.archives.state.al.us/referenc/family.html
www.geocities.com/Area51/Lair/3680/cw/cw-al.html
www.archives.state.al.us/
http://pilot.familysearch.org/recordsearch/start.html#p=0
www.familysearch.org
www.heritagequestonline.com
www.ancestry.com

www.footnote.com
PeopleFinders.com
www.lib.auburn.edu/sca/search.html
www.archives.state.al.us/referenc/hsglist.html
www.genealinks.com/states/al.htm
CriminalSearches.com
Intelius.com
Peoplescanner.com
www.daddezio.com/society/hill/SH-AL-NDX.html

Alaska

www.rootsweb.com/roots-l/USA/ak.html
www.akgenweb.org/
www.interment.net/us/ak/index.htm
GenealogyBank.com
www.archives.state.ak.us/
www.footnote.com
PeopleFinders.com
www.archives.gov/facilities/ak/anchorage.html
www.daddezio.com/society/hill/SH-AK-NDX.html
http://pilot.familysearch.org/recordsearch/start.html#p=0
www.familysearch.org
www.heritagequestonline.com
www.ancestry.com
CriminalSearches.com
Intelius.com
Peoplescanner.com
http://www.archives.state.ak.us/genealogy/genealogy.html

Arizona

www.rootsweb.com/roots-l/USA/az.html
http://www.azlibrary.gov/is/genealogy/index.cfm
GenealogyBank.com
www.lib.az.us/Bio/index.cfm
http://pilot.familysearch.org/recordsearch/start.html#p=0
www.familysearch.org
www.heritagequestonline.com
www.ancestry.com
www.footnote.com
PeopleFinders.com
www.interment.net/us/az/index.htm
CriminalSearches.com
Intelius.com
Peoplescanner.com
www.daddezio.com/society/hill/SH-AZ-NDX.html

Arkansas

www.argenweb.net
http://www.state.ar.us/family_gen.php
www.southwestarchives.com
www.rootsweb.com/~usgenweb/ar/arfiles.htm
www.rootsweb.com/~usgenweb/ar/search.htm
GenealogyBank.com
www.argenweb.net/arcounty.htm
http://searches.rootsweb.com/cgi-bin/arkland/arkland.pl
http://pilot.familysearch.org/recordsearch/start.html#p=0
www.familysearch.org
www.heritagequestonline.com
www.ancestry.com

www.footnote.com
PeopleFinders.com
www.interment.net/us/ar/index.htm
www.geocities.com/Area51/Lair/3680/cw/cw-ar.html
www.ark-ives.com/
www.southwestarchives.com/
http://anpa.ualr.edu/finding_aids/collection_finding_aids.htm
CriminalSearches.com
Intelius.com
Peoplescanner.com
www.daddezio.com/society/hill/SH-AR-NDX.html

California

http://cagenweb.com
www.interment.net/us/ca/index.htm
www.berkeleypubliclibrary.org/system/histrm.html
GenealogyBank.com
http://www2.anaheim.net/article.cfm?id=113
www.californiahistoricalsociety.org/collections/
    research_coll.html
http://www.library.ca.gov/calhist/genealogy.html
www.ss.ca.gov/archives/archives.htm
www.csrmf.org/doc.asp?id=122
www.csudh.edu/archives/csu/index.html
www.lapl.org/central/history.html
www.library.sfsu.edu/special/archives1.html
http://pilot.familysearch.org/recordsearch/start.html#p=0
www.familysearch.org
www.heritagequestonline.com
www.ancestry.com
www.footnote.com

PeopleFinders.com
www.californiapioneers.org/
www.library.ucla.edu/libraries/special/scweb/archives.htm
www.usfca.edu/library/archives.html
www.usc.edu/isd/archives/arc/libraries/index.html
CriminalSearches.com
Intelius.com
Peoplescanner.com
www.daddezio.com/society/hill/SH-CA-NDX.html

Colorado

http://cogenweb.com
http://www.colorado.gov/dpa/doit/archives/geneal.htm
GenealogyBank.com
www.interment.net/us/co/index.htm
www.coloradohistory.org/chs_library/library.htm
www.colorado.gov/dpa/doit/archives/
www.archives.gov/facilities/co/denver.html
http://ucblibraries.colorado.edu/archives/index.htm
http://pilot.familysearch.org/recordsearch/start.html#p=0
www.familysearch.org
www.heritagequestonline.com
www.ancestry.com
www.footnote.com
PeopleFinders.com
CriminalSearches.com
Intelius.com
Peoplescanner.com
www.daddezio.com/society/hill/SH-CO-NDX.html

Connecticut

http://www.cslib.org/starting.htm
http://www.ctgenweb.org
www.interment.net/us/ct/index.htm
www.newenglandancestors.org/research/Database/great
Migrations/default.asp
GenealogyBank.com
www.chs.org/library/
www.cslib.org/archives.htm
http://oldsaybrook.com/History/research.htm
www.lib.uconn.edu/online/research/speclib/ASC/
http://pilot.familysearch.org/recordsearch/start.html#p=0
www.familysearch.org
www.ancestry.com
www.heritagequestonline.com
www.footnote.com
PeopleFinders.com
www.library.yale.edu/mssa/
CriminalSearches.com
Intelius.com
Peoplescanner.com
www.daddezio.com/society/hill/SH-CT-NDX.html

Delaware

www.degenweb.org
www.interment.net/us/de/index.htm
www.state.de.us/sos/dpa/
www.hsd.org/library.htm
http://www.hsd.org/gengd.htm
GenealogyBank.com

www.udel.edu/Archives/
http://delgensoc.org/delrep.html
http://pilot.familysearch.org/recordsearch/start.html#p=0
www.familysearch.org
www.ancestry.com
www.heritagequestonline.com
www.footnote.com
PeopleFinders.com
CriminalSearches.com
Intelius.com
Peoplescanner.com
www.daddezio.com/society/hill/SH-DE-NDX.html

District of Columbia

www.interment.net/us/dc/index.htm
http://carnegieinstitution.org/legacy/default.html
GenealogyBank.com
http://www.dar.org/library/speccol.cfm
http://os.dc.gov/os/cwp/view,A,1207,Q,585889.asp
www.loc.gov/rr/mss/
www7.nationalacademies.org/archives/
http://pilot.familysearch.org/recordsearch/start.html#p=0
www.familysearch.org
www.ancestry.com
www.heritagequestonline.com
www.footnote.com
PeopleFinders.com
www.nmnh.si.edu/naa/about.htm
www.archives.gov/index.html
CriminalSearches.com
Intelius.com

Peoplescanner.com
http://siarchives.si.edu/

Florida

www.interment.net/us/fl/index.htm
http://dlis.dos.state.fl.us/library/Bibliographies/genealogy.cfm
http://dlis.dos.state.fl.us/barm/
GenealogyBank.com
www.library.miami.edu/archives/intro.html
http://pilot.familysearch.org/recordsearch/start.html#p=0
www.familysearch.org
www.ancestry.com
www.heritagequestonline.com
www.footnote.com
PeopleFinders.com
CriminalSearches.com
Intelius.com
Peoplescanner.com
www.daddezio.com/society/hill/SH-FL-NDX.html

Georgia

www.theclearances.org/clearances/destinations.php?
    placeid=61
www.rootsweb.com/~gagenweb
www.interment.net/us/ga/index.htm
http://www.georgia.gov/00/channel_title/
    0,2094,4802_13153498,00.html
GenealogyBank.com
www.atlantahistorycenter.com/
www.af.public.lib.ga.us/aarl/index.html

www.georgiaarchives.org/
www.archives.gov/facilities/ga/atlanta.html
www.libs.uga.edu/hargrett/speccoll.html
http://pilot.familysearch.org/recordsearch/start.html#p=0
www.familysearch.org
www.ancestry.com
www.heritagequestonline.com
www.footnote.com
PeopleFinders.com
CriminalSearches.com
Intelius.com
Peoplescanner.com
www.daddezio.com/society/hill/SH-GA-NDX.html

Hawaii

www.rootsweb.com/~higenweb/hawaii.htm
http://hawaii.gov/health/vital-records/vital-records/
    genealogy.html
GenealogyBank.com
www.interment.net/us/hi/index.htm
www.mauimuseum.org/archives1.html
www.punahou.edu/libraries/Archives/
http://pilot.familysearch.org/recordsearch/start.html#p=0
www.familysearch.org
www.ancestry.com
www.heritagequestonline.com
www.footnote.com
PeopleFinders.com
CriminalSearches.com
Intelius.com
Peoplescanner.com
www.daddezio.com/society/hill/SH-HI-NDX.html

Idaho

http://www.idahohistory.net/library_collections.html
GenealogyBank.com
www.rootsweb.com/~idgenweb/
www.interment.net/us/id/index.htm
www.idahohistory.net/library_archives.html
www.lib.uidaho.edu/special-collections/
http://pilot.familysearch.org/recordsearch/start.html#p=0
www.familysearch.org
www.ancestry.com
www.heritagequestonline.com
www.footnote.com
PeopleFinders.com
CriminalSearches.com
Intelius.com
Peoplescanner.com
www.daddezio.com/society/hill/SH-ID-NDX.html

Illinois

http://www.sos.state.il.us/departments/archives/services.html
www.interment.net/us/id/index.htm
www.evanstonhistorical.org/archives.html
www.cyberdriveillinois.com/departments/archives/
    archives.html
www.newberry.org/genealogy/L3gabout.html
http://www.cookcountygenealogy.com/
GenealogyBank.com
www.library.northwestern.edu/spec/
www.skokiehistory.info/genealog.html
http://pilot.familysearch.org/recordsearch/start.html#p=0

www.familysearch.org
www.heritagequestonline.com
http://www.edwardsvillelibrary.org/online-databases/
www.ancestry.com
www.footnote.com
PeopleFinders.com
www.rootsweb.com/~ilsgs/index.html
www.bsu.edu/library/collections/archives/
CriminalSearches.com
Intelius.com
Peoplescanner.com
www.daddezio.com/society/hill/SH-IL-NDX.html

Indiana

www.ingenweb.org/
http://www.acpl.lib.in.us/genealogy/index.html
www.interment.net/us/in/index.htm
GenealogyBank.com
http://friendsofallencounty.org/fwacdb.php
http://friendsofallencounty.org/
www.legion.org/?section=community&subsection=
    com_library&content=com_lib_collection
www.indianahistory.org/library/collections.html
http://pilot.familysearch.org/recordsearch/start.html#p=0
http://www.indgensoc.org/membersonly/databases.php
www.familysearch.org
www.ancestry.com
www.heritagequestonline.com
www.footnote.com
PeopleFinders.com
CriminalSearches.com

Intelius.com
Peoplescanner.com
www.daddezio.com/society/hill/SH-IN-NDX.html

Iowa

http://iagenweb.org/
http://www.iowahistory.org/library/family_history/
    research_tips.html
GenealogyBank.com
www.interment.net/us/ia/index.htm
www.iowahistory.org/archives/index.html
http://pilot.familysearch.org/recordsearch/start.html#p=0
www.familysearch.org
www.ancestry.com
www.heritagequestonline.com
www.footnote.com
PeopleFinders.com
CriminalSearches.com
Intelius.com
Peoplescanner.com
www.daddezio.com/society/hill/SH-IA-NDX.html

Kansas

http://www.kshs.org/genealogists/index.htm
http://skyways.lib.ks.us/genweb/index.html
www.interment.net/us/ks/index.htm
GenealogyBank.com
http://www.kansasmemory.org/
www.odessa3.org/collections/land/kansas/
www.fhsu.edu/forsyth_lib/arch.shtml

www.kshs.org/places/chr/index.htm
www.lib.ksu.edu/depts/spec/
http://skyways.lib.ks.us/kansas/genweb/mhgs/
    mhgs_library.htm
http://pilot.familysearch.org/recordsearch/start.html#p=0
www.familysearch.org
www.ancestry.com
www.heritagequestonline.com
www.footnote.com
PeopleFinders.com
CriminalSearches.com
Intelius.com
Peoplescanner.com
www.daddezio.com/society/hill/SH-KS-NDX.html

Kentucky

http://kdla.ky.gov/researchlinks/genealogy.htm
www.kygenweb.net/index.html
www.interment.net/us/ky/index.htm
GenealogyBank.com
www.kybaptist.org/kbc/welcome.nsf/pages/
    ExecutiveArchives
http://sos.ky.gov/land/search/default.htm
http://pilot.familysearch.org/recordsearch/start.html#p=0
www.familysearch.org
www.heritagequestonline.com
www.ancestry.com
www.footnote.com
PeopleFinders.com
CriminalSearches.com
Intelius.com

Peoplescanner.com
www.daddezio.com/society/hill/SH-KY-NDX.html

Louisiana

www.ibiblio.org/laslave/fields.php
http://searches.rootsweb.com/cgi-bin/laland/laland.pl
GenealogyBank.com
www.lagenweb.org/
www.clickers.org/genealogy/louisian.html
www.rootsweb.com/roots-l/USA/la.html
www.interment.net/us/la/index.htm
www.sec.state.la.us/archives/archives/archives-index.htm
www.youngsanders.org/page3.html
www.notarialarchives.org/
www.state.lib.la.us/la_dyn_templ.cfm?doc_id=114
http://www.state.lib.la.us/la_dyn_templ.cfm?doc_id=279
http://www.msa.md.gov/msa/refserv/genealogy/html/
    genstart.html
http://www.nsula.edu/creole/
www.xula.edu/library/archives.html
http://pilot.familysearch.org/recordsearch/start.html#p=0
www.familysearch.org
www.heritagequestonline.com
www.ancestry.com
www.footnote.com
PeopleFinders.com
CriminalSearches.com
Intelius.com
Peoplescanner.com
www.daddezio.com/society/hill/SH-LA-NDX.html

Maine

http://upperstjohn.com/aroostook/deane-kavanagh.htm
http://www.maine.gov/portal/facts_history/genealogy.html
http://upperstjohn.com/1820/index.htm
www.rootsweb.com/~megenweb/
GenealogyBank.com
www.interment.net/us/me/index.htm
www.newenglandancestors.org/research/Database/
    cemeteries/default.asp
www.mainehistory.org/library_overview.shtml
www.state.me.us/sos/arc/
www.umfk.maine.edu/archives/
http://acim.umfk.maine.edu/
http://pilot.familysearch.org/recordsearch/start.html#p=0
www.familysearch.org
www.ancestry.com
www.heritagequestonline.com
www.footnote.com
PeopleFinders.com
CriminalSearches.com
Intelius.com
Peoplescanner.com
www.daddezio.com/society/hill/SH-ME-NDX.html

Maryland

www.mdgenweb.org/
www.interment.net/us/md/index.htm
www.borail.org/resources/archives_library.asp
GenealogyBank.com
www.lib.umd.edu/LAB/

www.mdhs.org/library/library.html
www.mdarchives.state.md.us
www.archives.gov/facilities/md/archives_2.html
www.lib.umd.edu/ARCV/
http://pilot.familysearch.org/recordsearch/start.html#p=0
www.familysearch.org
www.ancestry.com
www.heritagequestonline.com
www.footnote.com
PeopleFinders.com
CriminalSearches.com
Intelius.com
Peoplescanner.com
www.daddezio.com/society/hill/SH-MD-NDX.html

Massachusetts

http://www.sec.state.ma.us/arc/arcgen/genidx.htm
www.rootsweb.com/~magenweb/
www.interment.net/us/ma/index.htm
www.americanantiquarian.org/digital2.htm
GenealogyBank.com
http://hul.harvard.edu/huarc/
www.huri.harvard.edu/library.coll.html
www.masshist.org/library/
www.sec.state.ma.us/arc/arcidx.htm
www.nha.org/library/genealogy.html
www.archives.gov/northeast/pittsfield/pittsfield.html
www.archives.gov/northeast/waltham/waltham.html
www.newenglandancestors.org/
www.mass.gov/lib/collections/sc.htm
www.milnelibrary.org/hlh.html

http://pilot.familysearch.org/recordsearch/start.html#p=0
www.familysearch.org
www.ancestry.com
www.heritagequestonline.com
www.footnote.com
PeopleFinders.com
CriminalSearches.com
Intelius.com
Peoplescanner.com
www.daddezio.com/society/hill/SH-MA-NDX.html

Michigan

www.rootsweb.com/~mistcla2/
www.rootsweb.com/~migenweb/
www.interment.net/us/mi/index.htm
http://bentley.umich.edu/
GenealogyBank.com
http://clarke.cmich.edu/
www.detroit.lib.mi.us/E_Resources/E-
    Resources_BurtonHistorical.htm
www.dsgr.org/
http://www.mcpl.lib.mo.us/genlh/
http://fchsm.habitant.org/
www.rootsweb.com/%7Emiigsm/
www.pgsm.org/
www.michigan.gov/hal/0,1607,7-160-15481_19271_
    21347—-,00.html
www.msu.edu/unit/msuarhc/collections.htm
GenealogyBank.com
www.michigan.gov/hal/0,1607,7-160-17445_19273_
    19313—-,00.html

www.umich.edu/~bhl/bhl/refhome/genie.htm
www.wmich.edu/library/archives/index.php
http://pilot.familysearch.org/recordsearch/start.html#p=0
www.familysearch.org
http://quod.lib.umich.edu/m/micounty/
www.ancestry.com
www.heritagequestonline.com
www.footnote.com
PeopleFinders.com
CriminalSearches.com
Intelius.com
Peoplescanner.com
www.daddezio.com/society/hill/SH-MI-NDX.html

Minnesota

www.rootsweb.com/~mngenweb/
http://www.mnhs.org/genealogy/
GenealogyBank.com
www.interment.net/us/mn/index.htm
www.mnhs.org/collections/library/library.htm
http://special.lib.umn.edu/rare/
http://pilot.familysearch.org/recordsearch/start.html#p=0
www.familysearch.org
www.ancestry.com
www.heritagequestonline.com
www.footnote.com
PeopleFinders.com
CriminalSearches.com
Intelius.com
Peoplescanner.com
http://www.daddezio.com/society/hill/SH-MN-NDX.html

Mississippi

www.interment.net/us/ms/index.htm
http://www.mdah.state.ms.us/admin/all_societies.html
http://lauderdalecounty.org/archivespage2.htm
www.mdah.state.ms.us
GenealogyBank.com
www.olemiss.edu/depts/general_library/files/archives/
    index.html
www.lib.usm.edu/~archives/
http://pilot.familysearch.org/recordsearch/start.html#p=0
www.familysearch.org
www.ancestry.com
www.heritagequestonline.com
www.footnote.com
PeopleFinders.com
CriminalSearches.com
Intelius.com
Peoplescanner.com
www.daddezio.com/society/hill/SH-MS-NDX.html

Missouri

www.rootsweb.com/~mogenweb/mo.htm
http://www.sos.mo.gov/archives/resources/links.asp
www.interment.net/us/mo/index.htm
www.nazarene.org/archives/index.html
www.mohistory.org/content/LibraryAndResearch/
    LRCGeneralInfo.aspx
GenealogyBank.com
www.archives.gov/facilities/mo/kansas_city.html
www.archives.gov/facilities/mo/st_louis.html

http://bav.vatican.va/en/v_home_bav/v_storia/index.shtml
www.umkc.edu/whmckc
http://pilot.familysearch.org/recordsearch/start.html#p=0
www.familysearch.org
www.ancestry.com
www.heritagequestonline.com
www.footnote.com
PeopleFinders.com
CriminalSearches.com
Intelius.com
Peoplescanner.com
www.daddezio.com/society/hill/SH-MS-NDX.html

Montana

http://www.montanahistoricalsociety.org/research/library/
    genealogyresearch.asp
GenealogyBank.com
www.rootsweb.com/~mtgenweb
www.interment.net/us/mt/index.htm
www.lewisandclark.org/?p=lib_arc&n=lib_arc
http://montanahistoricalsociety.org/research/library/aboutus.asp
http://pilot.familysearch.org/recordsearch/start.html#p=0
www.familysearch.org
www.ancestry.com
www.heritagequestonline.com
www.footnote.com
PeopleFinders.com
CriminalSearches.com
Intelius.com
Peoplescanner.com
www.daddezio.com/society/hill/SH-MT-NDX.html

Nebraska

http://negenweb.org/
http://www.hhs.state.ne.us/ced/genealog.htm
www.GenealogyBank.com
www.interment.net/us/ne/index.htm
www.nebraskahistory.org/lib-arch/index.htm
http://pilot.familysearch.org/recordsearch/start.html#p=0
www.familysearch.org
www.ancestry.com
www.heritagequestonline.com
www.footnote.com
PeopleFinders.com
CriminalSearches.com
Intelius.com
Peoplescanner.com
www.daddezio.com/society/hill/SH-NE-NDX.html

Nevada

http://www.statearchives.us/nevada.htm
http://www.nvgenweb.org/
GenealogyBank.com
www.interment.net/us/nv/index.htm
http://pilot.familysearch.org/recordsearch/start.html#p=0
www.familysearch.org
www.ancestry.com
www.heritagequestonline.com
www.footnote.com
PeopleFinders.com
CriminalSearches.com
Intelius.com

Peoplescanner.com
www.daddezio.com/society/hill/SH-NV-NDX.html

New Hampshire

http://www.nh.gov/nhsl/services/public/genealogy.html
www.usroots.com/%7Eusgwnhus/
GenealogyBank.com
www.interment.net/us/nh/index.htm
http://www.dartmouth.edu/~library/rauner/
www.nhhistory.org/specialcollections.html
www.state.nh.us/nhsl/history/index.html
http://pilot.familysearch.org/recordsearch/start.html#p=0
www.familysearch.org
www.ancestry.com
www.heritagequestonline.com
www.footnote.com
PeopleFinders.com
CriminalSearches.com
Intelius.com
Peoplescanner.com
www.daddezio.com/society/hill/SH-NH-NDX.html

New Jersey

http://www.njarchives.org/links/webcat/genealogy.html
www.njgenweb.org/
GenealogyBank.com
www.interment.net/us/nj/index.htm
www.jerseyhistory.org/archivesmain.html
www.state.nj.us/state/darm/links/archives.html
www.princeton.edu/~rbsc/

www.libraries.rutgers.edu/rul/libs/scua/genealogy/
    genealogy.shtml
http://pilot.familysearch.org/recordsearch/start.html#p=0
www.familysearch.org
www.ancestry.com
www.heritagequestonline.com
www.footnote.com
PeopleFinders.com
CriminalSearches.com
Intelius.com
Peoplescanner.com
www.daddezio.com/society/hill/SH-NJ-NDX.html

New Mexico

http://www.nmcpr.state.nm.us/archives/ancestors.htm
GenealogyBank.com
http://www.nmgenweb.us/
www.interment.net/us/nm/index.htm
http://archives.nmsu.edu/
www.unm.edu/~unmarchv/unmarchv.html
http://pilot.familysearch.org/recordsearch/start.html#p=0
www.familysearch.org
www.ancestry.com
www.heritagequestonline.com
www.footnote.com
PeopleFinders.com
CriminalSearches.com
Intelius.com
Peoplescanner.com
www.daddezio.com/society/hill/SH-NM-NDX.html

New York

www.rootsweb.com/~nygenweb/

http://www.archives.nysed.gov/a/research/res_topics_
genealogy.shtml

www.interment.net/us/ny/index.htm

http://www.newyorkancestors.org/

www.newenglandancestors.org/research/Database/
cemeteries/default.asp

http://query.nytimes.com/search/query?srchst=nyt&&srcht=
a&srchr=n

GenealogyBank.com

www.newyorkfamilyhistory.org

www.nypl.org

www.albanycounty.com/achor

www.buffalolib.org/libraries/collections/grosvenor.asp?
sec=genealogy

www.bechs.org/research.htm

www.cjh.org/academic

www.columbia.edu/cu/lweb/indiv/rbml/

http://rmc.library.cornell.edu/

www.liu.edu/cwis/cwp/library/sc/sc.htm

www.morganlibrary.org/collections/default.asp

www.archives.gov/northeast/nyc/new_york.html

www.newyorkfamilyhistory.org/modules.php?name=
Content&pa=showpage&pid=10

www.archives.nysed.gov/aindex.shtml

www.nysha.org/library/special_collections/

http://ny-genes.blogspot.com/

www.nysl.nysed.gov/mssdesc.htm

http://library.nyu.edu/collections/archives.html

www.nyu.edu/library/bobst/research/aia/

http://library.albany.edu/speccoll/
www.lib.rochester.edu/rbk/rarehome.htm
http://pilot.familysearch.org/recordsearch/start.html#p=0
www.familysearch.org
www.ancestry.com
www.heritagequestonline.com
www.footnote.com
PeopleFinders.com
CriminalSearches.com
Intelius.com
Peoplescanner.com
www.daddezio.com/society/hill/SH-NY-NDX.html

North Carolina

www.rootsweb.com/~ncgenweb
www.interment.net/us/nc/index.htm
www.library.appstate.edu/appcoll/genealogy.html
GenealogyBank.com
http://scriptorium.lib.duke.edu/
www.ah.dcr.state.nc.us/archives/
www.ah.dcr.state.nc.us/archives/OBHC/default.htm
http://library.uncg.edu/depts/speccoll/
http://www.accessgenealogy.com/northcarolina/index.htm
www.wfu.edu/Library/special/index.html
http://pilot.familysearch.org/recordsearch/start.html#p=0
www.familysearch.org
www.ancestry.com
www.heritagequestonline.com
www.footnote.com
PeopleFinders.com
CriminalSearches.com

Intelius.com
Peoplescanner.com
www.daddezio.com/society/hill/SH-NC-NDX.html

North Dakota

http://www.nd.gov/hist/sal/gen.htm
www.rootsweb.com/~ndgenweb/
GenealogyBank.com
www.interment.net/us/nd/index.htm
www.odessa3.org/collections/cemeteries/nodak/
www.odessa3.org/collections/census/
www.odessa3.org/collections/land/nodak/
www.state.nd.us/hist/sal.htm
http://pilot.familysearch.org/recordsearch/start.html#p=0
www.familysearch.org
www.ancestry.com
www.heritagequestonline.com
www.footnote.com
PeopleFinders.com
CriminalSearches.com
Intelius.com
Peoplescanner.com
www.daddezio.com/society/hill/SH-ND-NDX.html

Ohio

http://www.columbuslibrary.org/ebranch/index.cfm?pageid=
    69&parentid=481
www.rootsweb.com/~ohgenweb/
www.interment.net/us/oh/index.htm
www.americanjewisharchives.org/aja/general/no_flash.html

GenealogyBank.com
http://library.case.edu/ksl/speccoll/collections.html
http://library.cincymuseum.org/
www.erielackhs.org/ELHS/ELHSArchives.html
www.ohiohistory.org/resource/statearc/index.html
http://library.osu.edu/sites/archives/
www.libraries.uc.edu/libraries/arb/index.html
http://pilot.familysearch.org/recordsearch/start.html#p=0
www.familysearch.org
www.ancestry.com
www.heritagequestonline.com
www.footnote.com
PeopleFinders.com
CriminalSearches.com
Intelius.com
Peoplescanner.com
www.daddezio.com/society/hill/SH-OH-NDX.html

Oklahoma

http://www.odl.state.ok.us/oar/resources/genealogy.htm
http://www.okgenweb.org/
www.rootsweb.com/~itgenweb/
GenealogyBank.com
www.interment.net/us/ok/index.htm
http://library.nsuok.edu/Archives/index.html
www.odl.state.ok.us/oar/index2.htm
www-lib.ou.edu/info/index.asp?id=22
http://pilot.familysearch.org/recordsearch/start.html#p=0
www.familysearch.org
www.ancestry.com
www.heritagequestonline.com

www.footnote.com
PeopleFinders.com
CriminalSearches.com
Intelius.com
Peoplescanner.com
www.daddezio.com/society/hill/SH-OK-NDX.html

Oregon

http://arcweb.sos.state.or.us/banners/genealogy.htm
GenealogyBank.com
www.rootsweb.com/~orgenweb/
www.interment.net/us/or/index.htm
www.newportnet.com/coasthistory/Research.htm
http://arcweb.sos.state.or.us/
http://osulibrary.oregonstate.edu/archives/
www.sohs.org/Page.asp?NavID=43
http://pilot.familysearch.org/recordsearch/start.html#p=0
www.familysearch.org
www.ancestry.com
www.heritagequestonline.com
www.footnote.com
PeopleFinders.com
CriminalSearches.com
Intelius.com
Peoplescanner.com
www.daddezio.com/society/hill/SH-OR-NDX.html

Pennsylvania

http://www.portal.state.pa.us/portal/server.pt?open=
    512&mode=2&objID=1426

www.pagenweb.org/
www.interment.net/us/pa/index.htm
www.abc-usa.org/abhs
GenealogyBank.com
www.mercermuseum.org/spruancelibrary/index.html
www.lancasterhistory.org/research/services.html
www.archives.gov/midatlantic/public_services/
    public_services.html
www.hbg.psu.edu/library/libamc.html
www.phmc.state.pa.us/bah/dam/overview.htm?secid=31
www.phila.gov/phils/carchive.htm
http://library.temple.edu/collections/urbana/
http://carlisle-www.army.mil/usamhi/
www.library.pitt.edu/libraries/special/special.html
www.hsp.org/
www.hsp.org/default.aspx?id=2
http://pilot.familysearch.org/recordsearch/start.html#p=0
www.familysearch.org
www.ancestry.com
www.heritagequestonline.com
www.footnote.com
PeopleFinders.com
CriminalSearches.com
Intelius.com
Peoplescanner.com
http://www.daddezio.com/society/hill/SH-PA-NDX.html

Rhode Island

http://www.rigensoc.org/rigenresources.htm
GenealogyBank.com
www.rootsweb.com/~rigenweb/

www.interment.net/us/ri/index.htm

www.newenglandancestors.org/research/Database/
greatMigrations/default.asp

www.newenglandancestors.org/research/Database/
cemeteries/default.asp

www.afgs.org/afgsrsrc.html

www.brown.edu/Facilities/University_Library/libs/hay/
index.html

www.providenceathenaeum.org/services/speccoll.php

www.ric.edu/adamslibrary/resources/bibliographies/
capeverde.html

GenealogyBank.com

www.rihs.org/libraryhome.htm

http://www3.sec.state.ri.us/Archives/

www.courts.ri.gov/records/defaultrecords.htm

www.uri.edu/library/special_collections/

http://pilot.familysearch.org/recordsearch/start.html#p=0

www.familysearch.org

www.ancestry.com

www.heritagequestonline.com

www.footnote.com

PeopleFinders.com

CriminalSearches.com

Intelius.com

Peoplescanner.com

www.daddezio.com/society/hill/SH-RI-NDX.html

South Carolina

http://archives.sc.gov/genealogy/

www.geocities.com/Heartland/Hills/3837/?20058

www.interment.net/us/sc/index.htm

GenealogyBank.com
www.bju.edu/library/collections/spc.html
www.mindspring.com/~camdenarchives/index.html
www.ccpl.org/content.asp?catID=5402&parentID=5372
www.citadel.edu/archivesandmuseum/#archives
www.cofc.edu/avery
www.geocities.com/Heartland/Estates/7212/introduction.html
www.threerivershistoricalsociety.org
www.state.sc.us/scdah/research.htm
www.schistory.org/
www.sc.edu/library/socar/books.html
http://carolus.furman.edu/depts/speccoll/speccoll.htm
www.sc.edu/library/spcoll/rarebook.html
http://pilot.familysearch.org/recordsearch/start.html#p=0
www.familysearch.org
www.ancestry.com
www.heritagequestonline.com
www.footnote.com
PeopleFinders.com
CriminalSearches.com
Intelius.com
Peoplescanner.com
www.daddezio.com/society/hill/SH-SC-NDX.html

South Dakota

http://www.sdhistory.org/arc/arcgen.htm
http://sdgenweb.com/
GenealogyBank.com
www.interment.net/us/sd/index.htm
www.odessa3.org/collections/cemeteries/sodak
www.odessa3.org/collections/census

www.odessa3.org/collections/land/sodak
www.sdhistory.org/arc/archives.htm
www.usd.edu/library/special
http://pilot.familysearch.org/recordsearch/start.html#p=0
www.familysearch.org
www.ancestry.com
www.heritagequestonline.com
www.footnote.com
PeopleFinders.com
CriminalSearches.com
Intelius.com
Peoplescanner.com
www.daddezio.com/society/hill/SH-SD-NDX.html

Tennessee

http://www.tennessee.gov/tsla/history/index.htm
www.tngenweb.org
www.interment.net/us/tn/index.htm
http://library.cn.edu/baptarch.html
GenealogyBank.com
http://faculty.leeu.edu/~drc/
www.jmcl.tn.org/genealog.htm
www.lambuth.edu/academics/library/
    MemphisConferenceArchives.html
http://home.lorettotel.net/~lcarchives/archives.htm
www.lmunet.edu/museum/collection/scguides.htm
http://janus.mtsu.edu/
www.sbhla.org/
www.sumnertn.org/archives/default.htm
www.tennessee.gov/tsla/history/index.htm
http://exlibris.memphis.edu/about/depts/special/index.html

http://library.sewanee.edu/archives/index.html
http://www.library.vanderbilt.edu/speccol/
http://pilot.familysearch.org/recordsearch/start.html#p=0
www.familysearch.org
www.ancestry.com
www.heritagequestonline.com
www.footnote.com
PeopleFinders.com
CriminalSearches.com
Intelius.com
Peoplescanner.com
www.daddezio.com/society/hill/SH-TN-NDX.html

Texas

http://www.tsl.state.tx.us/arc/genfirst.html
www.rootsweb.com/~txgenweb/
GenealogyBank.com
www.interment.net/us/tx/index.htm
www.dallashistory.org/about/research.htm
www.ci.dallas.tx.us/cso/archives.shtml
www.drtl.org/
www.irvinglibrary.org/genealogy.html
www.archives.gov/facilities/tx/fort_worth.html
www.tsl.state.tx.us/shc/index.html
www.glo.state.tx.us/archives.html
www.tsl.state.tx.us/arc/
www.library.unt.edu/archives/default.htm
http://pilot.familysearch.org/recordsearch/start.html#p=0
www.familysearch.org
www.ancestry.com
www.heritagequestonline.com
www.footnote.com

PeopleFinders.com
CriminalSearches.com
Intelius.com
Peoplescanner.com
www.daddezio.com/society/hill/SH-TX-NDX.html

Utah

http://archives.utah.gov/research/guides/index.html
www.rootsweb.com/~utgenweb/index.html
www.interment.net/us/ut/index.htm
www.familysearch.org/Eng/Library/FHL/frameset_
    library.asp
GenealogyBank.com
http://historyresearch.utah.gov/
http://library.usu.edu/Specol/index.html
http://pilot.familysearch.org/recordsearch/start.html#p=0
www.familysearch.org
http://archives.utah.gov/digital/328.htm
www.ancestry.com
www.heritagequestonline.com
www.footnote.com
http://www.lib.byu.edu/subsutility/index.php?sid=16
PeopleFinders.com
CriminalSearches.com
Intelius.com
Peoplescanner.com
www.daddezio.com/society/hill/SH-UT-NDX.html

Vermont

http://vermont-archives.org/research/genealogy/gene.htm
http://home.att.net/~Local_History/VT_History.htm

www.interment.net/us/vt/index.htm
www.vermonthistory.org/msscoll.htm
http://vermont-archives.org/
GenealogyBank.com
www.norwich.edu/academics/library.html
http://maozi.middlebury.edu/SharingVTHistory/index.htm
http://pilot.familysearch.org/recordsearch/start.html#p=0
www.familysearch.org
www.ancestry.com
www.heritagequestonline.com
www.footnote.com
PeopleFinders.com
CriminalSearches.com
Intelius.com
Peoplescanner.com
www.daddezio.com/society/hill/SH-VT-NDX.html

Virginia

http://www.lva.lib.va.us/WHATWEHAVE/gene/index.htm
www.interment.net/us/va/index.htm
www.lva.lib.va.us/whatwehave
http://www.arlingtonva.us/Departments/Libraries/history/
    LibrariesHistoryLocalHistory.aspx
GenealogyBank.com
http://www.chesapeake.lib.va.us/Wallace/
    wallace_memorial_room.htm
http://sos.ky.gov/land/nonmilitary/
www.lib.virginia.edu/small/vhp
www.emu.edu/library/histlib.html
www.co.fairfax.va.us/library/branches/vr/default.htm
www.hamptonu.edu/museum/archives.htm

www.hrl.lib.state.va.us/handley/services.asp?p=76
www.lva.lib.va.us/whatwedo/archives/index.htm
http://memory.loc.gov/ammem/
www.mcu.usmc.mil/MCRCweb/Archive/default.htm
www.mountvernon.org/learn/collections/index.cfm/ss/38
www.npl.lib.va.us/sgm/oldlobby/archive.html
www.lib.odu.edu/special/index.htm
www.leesburgva.org/services/Library/Resources/
www.lib.virginia.edu/small/collections/mss.html
www.vahistorical.org/research/genealogy.htm
www.vmi.edu/archives/alumni.html
http://library.wlu.edu/details.asp?resID=104
www.vgs.org/
http://ajax.lva.lib.va.us/F/?func=file&file_name=
    find-b-clas29&local_base=CLAS29
www.civilwar.nps.gov/cwss/
http://library.wlu.edu/research/specialcollections/
http://pilot.familysearch.org/recordsearch/start.html#p=0
www.familysearch.org
www.ancestry.com
www.heritagequestonline.com
www.footnote.com
PeopleFinders.com
CriminalSearches.com
Intelius.com
Peoplescanner.com
www.daddezio.com/society/hill/SH-VA-NDX.html

Washington

http://www.secstate.wa.gov/history/genealogy.aspx
http://www.digitalarchives.wa.gov:80/

www.wagenweb.org/
www.interment.net/us/wa/index.htm
GenealogyBank.com
www.hqrl.com/
www.archives.gov/facilities/wa/seattle.html
www.cityofseattle.net/CityArchives/
http://sfhs.eget.net/archives.html
www.secstate.wa.gov/archives/
www.cwu.edu/~archives/
www.secstate.wa.gov/archives/archives_eastern.aspx
www.secstate.wa.gov/archives/archives_northwest.
    aspx?m=undefined
www.secstate.wa.gov/archives/archives_puget.aspx?
    m=undefined
www.secstate.wa.gov/archives/archives_southwest.aspx?
    m=undefined
www.wwu.edu/depts/recmgmt/
http://pilot.familysearch.org/recordsearch/start.html#p=0
www.familysearch.org
www.ancestry.com
www.heritagequestonline.com
www.footnote.com
PeopleFinders.com
CriminalSearches.com
Intelius.com
Peoplescanner.com
www.daddezio.com/society/hill/SH-WA-NDX.html

West Virginia

http://www.wvculture.org/history/genealog.html
www.interment.net/us/wv/index.htm

GenealogyBank.com
www.marshall.edu/speccoll/wvcoll.asp
www.wvculture.org/history/wvsamenu.html
www.libraries.wvu.edu/appalachian/
www.libraries.wvu.edu/wvcollection/index.htm
http://pilot.familysearch.org/recordsearch/start.html#p=0
www.familysearch.org
www.ancestry.com
www.heritagequestonline.com
www.footnote.com
PeopleFinders.com
CriminalSearches.com
Intelius.com
Peoplescanner.com
www.daddezio.com/society/hill/SH-WV-NDX.html

Wisconsin

http://wisconsinhistory.org/genealogy/
www.interment.net/us/wi/index.htm
GenealogyBank.com
www.dodgejeffgen.com/library.html
www.mpl.org/File/hum_milwroad_index.htm
http://archives.library.wisc.edu/
www.uwm.edu/Libraries/arch/division/
www.polishroots.org/heraldry.htm
www.wla.lib.wi.us/wiglhr/local.html
www.wisconsinhistory.org/libraryarchives/
http://pilot.familysearch.org/recordsearch/start.html#p=0
www.familysearch.org
www.ancestry.com
www.heritagequestonline.com

www.footnote.com
http://209.94.183.10/website/services_vdb.htm
PeopleFinders.com
CriminalSearches.com
Intelius.com
Peoplescanner.com
www.daddezio.com/society/hill/SH-WI-NDX.html

Wyoming

wygenweb.org
www.interment.net/us/wy/index.htm
www.jacksonholehistory.org/research.shtml
GenealogyBank.com
http://wyoarchives.state.wy.us/
http://ahc.uwyo.edu/default.htm
www.windriverhistory.org/washakiearchi.html
http://wyoarchives.state.wy.us/index.htm
http://pilot.familysearch.org/recordsearch/start.html#p=0
www.familysearch.org
www.ancestry.com
www.heritagequestonline.com
www.footnote.com
PeopleFinders.com
CriminalSearches.com
Intelius.com
Peoplescanner.com
www.daddezio.com/society/hill/SH-WY-NDX.html

Uruguay

www.world-newspapers.com

www.libdex.com/country.html
www.mec.gub.uy/agn
www.rau.edu.uy/universidad/ag/
www.apellidositalianos.com.ar/archivos_uruguayos.htm
http://members.aol.com/mrosado007/uruguay.htm
www.genealogienetz.de/reg/WELT/uruguay.html
http://lists.rootsweb.com/index/intl/URY/URUGUAY.html
http://vlib.iue.it/history/americas/Uruguay/
www.iegu.org.uy/
http://pilot.familysearch.org/recordsearch/start.html#p=0
www.familysearch.org

Uzbekistan

www.world-newspapers.com
www.libdex.com/country.html
http://vlib.iue.it/history/asia/Uzbekistan
http://lcweb2.loc.gov/frd/cs/uztoc.html
www.forumancientcoins.com/historia/islam_gen6.htm
www.cousinconnect.com/p/a/184/
http://pilot.familysearch.org/recordsearch/start.html#p=0
www.familysearch.org

Vanuatu

www.world-newspapers.com
www.vanuatu.usp.ac.fj/library/collections.htm#Special%
    20Collections
www.rootsweb.com/~melwgw/vanuatu
www.lonelyplanet.com/destinations/pacific/vanuatu/history.htm
http://home.att.net/~Local_Catholic/Catholic-Australia-
    Oceania.htm#Stillehavet

http://pilot.familysearch.org/recordsearch/start.html#p=0
www.familysearch.org

Vatican

www.world-newspapers.com
www.libdex.com/country.html
www.vatican.va/index.htm
http://bav.vatican.va/en/v_home_bav/home_bav.shtml
www.lib.utexas.edu/maps/europe/vaticancity.jpg
www.vatican.va/index.htm
www.vatican.va/library_archives/vat_secret_archives/coll
ections/index.htm
www.haaretz.com/hasen/objects/pages/PrintArticleEn.
    jhtml?itemNo=499571
http://pilot.familysearch.org/recordsearch/start.html#p=0
www.familysearch.org

Venezuela

www.world-newspapers.com
www.libdex.com/country.html
www.apellidositalianos.com.ar/archivos_venezolanos.htm
www.venezuelagenealogia.org
http://es.groups.yahoo.com/group/Venezuela_genealogia/
www.surnames.org/venezuel.htm
www.auyantepui.com/historia/index.shtml
http://freepages.genealogy.rootsweb.com/~venezuela/
    sp/sucre.html
http://freepages.genealogy.rootsweb.com/~tantagente/
http://buscador.infoguia.net/Sociedad/Genealogia/
www.orinoco.org/apg/loindex.asp?lang=en&first=true

http://pilot.familysearch.org/recordsearch/start.html#p=0
www.familysearch.org

Vietnam

www.world-newspapers.com
www.rootsweb.com/~vnmwgw/
www.archives.gov/research_room/research_topics/
    korea_and_vietnam_casualties.html
http://pilot.familysearch.org/recordsearch/start.html#p=0
www.familysearch.org

Virgin Islands (U.S.A.)

www.libdex.com/country.html
http://uvial.uvi.edu/imls/DeChabert/index.html
www.candoo.com
www.candoo.com/genresources/microfilms.htm
http://pilot.familysearch.org/recordsearch/start.html#p=0
www.familysearch.org

Volhynia
(See also Russia and Poland)

www.wolhynien.de
www.rootsweb.com/~ukrwgw/volynska
www.odessa3.org
www.jewishgen.org/ukraine/volhynia
www.inthemidstofwolves.com
www.sggee.org
http://pilot.familysearch.org/recordsearch/start.html#p=0
www.familysearch.org

Wales
(see also England and UK)

www.world-newspapers.com
www.libdex.com/country.html
http://pilot.familysearch.org/recordsearch/start.html#p=0
www.familysearch.org
www.ancestry.co.uk
www.rootsweb.com/~wlsafhs/index.htm
www.llgc.org.uk/cac/cac0023.htm
www.ull.ac.uk/his/introhis.html
www.oz.net/~markhow/welshros.htm
www.historicaldirectories.org/hd/findbylocation.asp
www.genuki.org.uk/big/wal
members.tripod.com/~Caryl_Williams/index-2.html
www.bbc.co.uk/wales/history/sites/familyhistory
www.clwydfhs.org.uk
www.uk-genealogy.org.uk/wales

West Prussia
(see also Poland and Germany)

www.genealogienetz.de/reg/WPRU/wprus.htm
http://www.vffow.de/default.htm
www.genealogienetz.de/vereine/AGoFF/index.htm
www.westpreussen.de
www.bundesarchiv.de
www.ezab.de
http://germanroots.home.att.net/putzig/
http://pilot.familysearch.org/recordsearch/start.html#p=0
www.familysearch.org

Western Sahara

www.world-newspapers.com
http://lists.rootsweb.com/index/intl/ESH/AFR-
   WESTERN-SAHARA.html
www.rootsweb.com/~nafrica/WESTERNSAHARA/
   SahraawiyGateway.html

Yemen

www.world-newspapers.com
www.uq.net.au/~zzhsoszy/files/gg_index.html
www.libdex.com/country.html
www.arab.net/yemen
www.forumancientcoins.com/historia/islam_gen5.htm
http://azaalcity.com/history.htm
http://pilot.familysearch.org/recordsearch/start.html#p=0
www.familysearch.org

Yugoslavia
(see Serbia and Montenegro)

Zambia
(previously Northern Rhodesia)

www.world-newspapers.com
http://lists.rootsweb.com/index/intl/ZMB/AFR-ZAMBIA.html
www.jewishgen.org/SAfrica/subcont.htm
www.statehouse.gov.zm
http://web.idrc.ca/es/ev-43016-201-1-DO_TOPIC.html
http://pilot.familysearch.org/recordsearch/start.html#p=0
www.familysearch.org

Zanzibar
(see also Tanzania)

www.uq.net.au/~zzhsoszy/files/gg_index.html
www.forumancientcoins.com/historia/islam_gen6.htm
www.amecea.org
www.casbah.ac.uk/newsarticle2.stm
http://www.wsu.edu:8080/%7Edee/CIVAFRCA/
    SWAHILI.HTM
http://archaeology.about.com/library/atlas/bltanzania.htm
http://www.pdavis.nl/Frere.htm
http://pilot.familysearch.org/recordsearch/start.html#p=0
www.familysearch.org

Zimbabwe
(previously Southern Rhodesia)

www.world-newspapers.com
www.libdex.com/country.html
www.uz.ac.zw/library/inner/specialcoll.html
www.bahai.co.zw
www.jewishgen.org/SAfrica/subcont.htm
www.africa-research.org/mainframe.html
http://pilot.familysearch.org/recordsearch/start.html#p=0
www.familysearch.org

Index